What Can
One Person Do?

What Can One Person Do?

Faith to Heal a Broken World

SABINA ALKIRE
and
EDMUND NEWELL

With Ann Barham,
Chloe Breyer, and Ian Douglas

CHURCH PUBLISHING
New York

A catalog record for this book is available from
the Library of Congress.

ISBN: 0-89869-498-1

Church Publishing Incorporated
445 Fifth Avenue
New York, NY 10016
www.churchpublishing.org

5 4 3 2 1

For Sarah Elizabeth Newell

Contents

Foreword

"Good news for the poor" is at the heart of Jesus' gospel. This wonderful book is for everyone who wants to share that good news but does not know where to begin.

Sabina Alkire, Edmund Newell, and their contributors point us in the right direction in two important ways. They not only suggest a whole range of practical steps; they also paint a vivid picture of what we are aiming for — a world where men, women, and children are freed from the dehumanizing conditions of extreme poverty and given the opportunity to transform their communities.

As the global community pursues the Millennium Development Goals, people everywhere have an unprecedented opportunity to contribute to their achievement. This book will tell you all you need to know about the MDGs and, whatever your interests or abilities, how you can help make a difference.

This book not only inspires us to act — it inspires us to believe that our goals are possible. Within its pages we find ourselves able to imagine a future where poverty is less, where relationships are just, and where, increasingly, global humanity shares equitably and sustainably the resources of our beautiful planet. As we come to see our own stories woven into the stories of our brothers and sisters around the world, we will learn to live out responsibly and joyfully our own place in this bigger picture of hope for all.

As you read this book, let yourself be inspired, to believe, and to act. There is nothing greater a human being can do than help change another person's life for the better.

The Most Reverend Njongonkulu Ndungane
Archbishop of Cape Town

Abbreviations

CAFOD	Catholic Agency for Overseas Development
ECUSA	Episcopal Church in the United States of America
EGR	Episcopalians for Global Reconciliation (*www.e4gr.org*)
G-8	Group of 8
GM	General Motors
GNI	Gross National Income
LC	Legislative Correspondent (US)
MDGs	Millennium Development Goals
MP	Member of Parliament (UK)
NGOs	Non-Governmental Organizations
NJB	New Jerusalem Bible
ODA	Overseas Development Assistance
UK	United Kingdom
US	United States
USAID	United States Agency for International Development

The Millennium Development Goals (MDGs)

In 2000, all the member states of the United Nations pledged to achieve eight goals by 2015. They said, "We will spare no effort to free our fellow men, women, and children from the abject and dehumanizing conditions of extreme poverty, to which more than a billion of them are now subjected." The goals, and where we are so far, are described below.

1. **Eradicate extreme poverty and hunger.** Specifically, the aim is by 2015 to reduce by half the proportion of people whose income in 1990 amounted to less than one US dollar a day, and reduce by half the proportion of people who were hungry.

   Currently 1.1 billion people live on less than one dollar a day, and 852 million are hungry.

2. **Achieve universal primary education.** The target is for all children — girls and boys alike — to be able to complete primary school.

   Currently 121 million school-aged children do not go to school.

3. **Promote gender equality and empower women.** The goal is for equal numbers of girls and boys to go to primary and secondary school by 2005 and go on to higher education by 2015.

   Currently 60 percent of the children out of school are girls.

4. **Reduce child mortality.** The aim is to reduce the rate of children who die before their fifth birthday by two-thirds by 2015.

   Currently 11 million children die of preventable diseases every year.

5. **Improve maternal health.** The target is to reduce maternal mortality by three-quarters.

   Currently around five hundred thousand mothers die each year of birth-related complications.

6. **Combat HIV/AIDS, malaria, and other diseases.** The goal is to reverse the spread of these dread diseases by 2015.

    Currently each year 3 million persons die of AIDS, nearly 2 million of tuberculosis, and 1 million of malaria.

7. **Ensure environmental sustainability.** The aims are to make drinking water safer and improve the lives of 100 million slum dwellers and reverse the loss of environmental resources.

    Currently 1.1 billion people lack access to a reliable source of water that is reasonably protected from contamination; 2.6 billion lack access to basic sanitation.

8. **Develop a global partnership for development.** The goal addresses a range of issues in which the developed countries play a particular role in inhibiting or facilitating poverty reduction. These include:

    * Ongoing debt relief and measures to make debt sustainable in the long term.

    * Trade and financial systems that promote good governance and poverty reduction.

    * Increasing the amount of good overseas development assistance to least developed countries to 0.7 percent of rich countries' and 0.15 percent of less developed countries' gross national income.

    * Access to affordable essential drugs, such as antiretrovirals.

    * Special attention to the needs of landlocked countries and small island states.

    * Strategies for decent and productive work for youth.

    * The sharing of information and communications technology.

Currently rich countries on average give 0.25 percent of their gross national income to development assistance; the goal is to increase this to 0.7 percent, of which over 0.5 percent goes to the MDGs.[1]

---

1. For a full list of indicators, see *www.developmentgoals.org/mdgun/MDG_metadata _08-01-03_UN.htm* or *http://millenniumindicators.un.org.*

Acknowledgments

We are very grateful for the wide range of comments and insights that have come from various drafts of this book. Members of Episcopalians for Global Reconciliation (EGR) read and gave opinions on the drafts. In Boston, groups at Trinity Church, Copley Square, and St. Stephen's Church, South End, discussed and commented on some chapters. A retreat group at St. Katharine's Foundation, London, gave feedback on some of this material. We are grateful to other friends and colleagues associated with EGR, particularly the initial organizers: the Rt. Rev. Jeffrey Rowthorn, the Rt. Rev. Arthur Walmsley, and Dr. Richard Parker. Ian Douglas expresses thanks to faculty colleagues at the Episcopal Divinity School who "continually challenge me as to my faithfulness to God's mission of justice, compassion, and reconciliation." We are also grateful for comments and help from Alex Baumgarten and Maureen Shea at the Episcopal Public Policy Network, Adrian and Sue Snell, Judith Radke, Carol Welch, Lallie Lloyd, Delene Mark, Tim Crellin, Claire Foster, Elizabeth Foy, Garth Hewitt, Hannah Alkire, Wendy Tyndale, Susan Newell, Kristin Douglas, Martin Warner, Alula Pankhurst, and to the Most Rev. Frank T. Griswold, presiding bishop of the Episcopal Church in the United States, for his leadership and commitment to God's mission of reconciliation.

The title and the suggestion of the Pontius Puddle cartoon came from Christy Risser-Milne, who also provided full and insightful suggestions on the first draft. Lucy Winkett put her library on feminist and liberation theologies at our disposal. Angus Ritchie, Pat Barham, and John Hammock gave patient and substantive comments on the entire draft. Michael Smitheram and other colleagues at Micah have provided detailed comments as well as forwarded materials to read and include. Craig Cole and Five Talents International provided comments as well as stories and newsletters. Daleep Mukarji, Charles Abugre, and others at Christian Aid provided a selection of human-interest stories. Muhammad Yunus and Ricardo Navarro each contributed a story.

We are grateful to Joel Kauffmann for permission to use his Pontius Puddle cartoon.

The authors kindly thank the following publishers for extending permission for the use of their materials in this volume. Every reasonable effort has been made to obtain appropriate permission for copyrighted materials. If you are a copyright holder and feel we have not obtained proper permission, please contact us and we will remedy the situation.

Christian Aid (*www.christianaid.org*)
The BBC World Service (*www.bbc.co.uk/worldservice/*)
Micah Challenge (*www.micahchallenge.org*)
Bread for the World (*www.bread.org*)
The United Nations (*www.un.org/millenniumgoals/*)
Reality of Aid (*www.realityofaid.org*)
The World Bank (*www.worldbank.org*)
Hunger and Public Action, edited by Jean Drèze and Amartya Sen
    (1991). By permission of Oxford University Press (*www.oup.com*)
Liberation Theology after the End of History, by Daniel Bell (2001).
    Used by permission of Taylor & Francis.
Excerpts from pp. 212 and 348 of *God's Politics: Why the Right Gets
    It Wrong and the Left Doesn't Get It,* by Jim Wallis. Copyright
    © 2004 by Jim Wallis. Reprinted by permission of HarperCollins
    Publishers.

Jonathan Reiber at Church Publishing Incorporated has displayed the keen blend of enthusiasm and patience that makes a writing project such as this enjoyable and energizing. Our interactions with Church Publishing Incorporated and Darton, Longman and Todd, through Virginia Hearn, have been very warm and constructive indeed.

This book is very much a collaborative effort. Ian Douglas contributed chapter 2, Chloe Breyer chapter 7, and Ann Barham drafted the actions at the end of each chapter. It has been an enriching experience to work together as a team, and we are also grateful to our families — those other team members — whose love and support has enabled this book to come to fruition.

Introduction

What Can One Person *Really* Do?

It is our conviction that there is much that one person, one family, one community, one minister, and one church can — and should — do to reduce global poverty. The Millennium Development Goals (MDGs), which will be discussed throughout this book, offer a unique opportunity for this generation to make a significant contribution to improve the lives of billions of people. Acting to support the MDGs offers a clear and practical answer to the question *What can one person do?* The aim of this book is to show how, and why, we should act.

"A vision without a task is boring. A task without a vision is awfully frustrating. A vision with a task can change the world."[1] These words, by Brizio Biondi-Morra, who runs a non-governmental organization (NGO) in Latin America, ring true. The vision and tasks developed here are not original. Yet perhaps if more people saw the vision and set about doing a few of these tasks regularly — and these are not really difficult — extreme poverty might be greatly reduced.

Who it's for

This book is for those who are concerned about global poverty and willing to work, speak, and act to reduce it. It is not aimed at a particular section of church or society, nor does it take up a strong position on the political spectrum. It may surprise you to hear this, but those on the left and right agree on many of the core tasks that are needed to reduce global poverty. It may also surprise you that many Christians also agree. In some places we Christians spend so much time honing and exercising our differences that we forget to claim our common ground. Arguments draw an audience, as press coverage on the divisions within the Anglican Communion proves. But if we gathered up most of the time and energy

---

1. In Katherine Marshall and Richard Marsh, eds., *Millennium Challenges for Development and Faith Institutions* (Washington, D.C.: World Bank, 2003), 63. Brizio Biondi-Morra is president of the AVINA Foundation, a Latin American organization working on sustainable development.

spent in bitter disputes and invested it in practicing core teachings, we might be of more service to the poor, and more faithful witnesses besides.

What is even better is that we don't discover our common ground by relegating our faith and scriptures and traditions and spiritual lives to the sidelines. We discover it by going back to these sources repeatedly, like a deer to a stream. The heart of Christian faith is intermingled with economic justice and concern for the poor. Did you know that Roman Catholic liberation theologians, biblical scholars, evangelical ministers, Mennonites, and even Nietzsche all agree that the New Testament places special emphasis on the poor and marginalized?

So wherever you place yourself on the political spectrum, whether you're a young student or middle-aged or retired, whether you love an-cient choral music or gospel or praise bands or contemplative silence, or whether you're reading this book for its views on poverty reduc-tion rather than Christianity, please know that you are welcomed and respected as a reader.

What is proposed?

To respond to the question *What can one person do?* this book highlights seven actions that, after quite thorough reflection, seem to be strategic. What surprised us might surprise you, so let us explain right away why we chose them. Some of these are the same actions that we've been hearing about since childhood. They seemed rather underwhelming and uninspiring to start with, while we wanted to be new and different. But when we went back to the evidence we learned something: if used with strategic cunning these actions *can be* important and will make a differ-ence. In the text we explain when each action is strategic so you know precisely why we've chosen it and when and how to do it. The actions are not in order of importance, for they cannot be ranked, but in order of appearance:

1. **Pray.** Hold people and situations in prayer.

2. **Study.** Lead a study group or discussion group on poverty using this book or another.

3. **Give.** Give 0.7 percent of your income toward the MDGs and teach others to do so.

4. **Connect.** Spend time abroad volunteering or visiting to connect with the impoverished.

5. **Raise Awareness.** Organize a concert or other public event to raise awareness and funds.

6. **Take Action.** Take part in a direct action — e.g., wear a white band.

7. **Advocate.** Write to, or meet, your government representatives to urge them to address global poverty.

Maybe these are not *new*, but when enough people do them they have worked in the past, and they will again. But please don't mistake this list for an answer to the title question. Each of us must discern and decide our own responses, year in and year out. Yours may vary quite a bit from these. To underscore this, the eighth "action" is actually a shower of suggestions that identify variations and alternative actions that might be more appropriate or attractive to some.

Public outcry

The Epistle of James challenges Christians to exert their faith in the social sphere:

> What good is it, my brothers and sisters, if you say you have faith but do not have works? Can faith save you? If a brother or sister is naked and lacks daily food, and one of you says to them, "Go in peace; keep warm and eat your fill," and yet you do not supply their bodily needs, what is the good of that? So faith by itself, if it has no works, is dead. (James 2:14–17)

Throughout history, faith groups have frequently taken a lead in championing the cause of the impoverished and marginalized, as well as providing practical help and resources to alleviate suffering. But the very fact that extreme poverty is so pervasive today indicates the need to reduce its magnitude and to align our efforts with one another. "More of the same" is morally untenable.

The eight Millennium Development Goals resonate powerfully with the Christian faith. The "Micah Call" printed below describes beautifully the link between our faith, the MDGs, and public action — and calls on Christians to respond:

The Micah Call

This is a moment in history of unique potential,
when the stated intentions of world leaders
echo something of the mind of the Biblical prophets
and the teachings of Jesus concerning the poor,
and when we have the means to dramatically reduce poverty.

We commit ourselves, as followers of Jesus,

to work together for the holistic transformation of our
     communities,
to pursue justice, be passionate about kindness, and to walk
     humbly with God.

We call on international and national decision-makers
of both rich and poor nations, to fulfil their public promise
to achieve the Millennium Development Goals
and so halve absolute global poverty by 2015.

We call on Christians everywhere to be agents of hope
for and with the poor, and to work with others
to hold our national and global leaders accountable
in securing a more just and merciful world.[2]

Thinking pragmatically, there is another reason to act, and it's equally compelling: feasibility. Experts in poverty reduction are *absolutely* baffled by why more people who hold strong moral values — of any religious faith or none — are *not* feeling compassion for the plight of the poor and acting energetically to address it, *because it is possible to do so.* The Nobel Prize–winning economist Amartya Sen and his India-based colleague Jean Drèze put it like this:

The persistence of widespread hunger is one of the most appalling features of the modern world. The fact that so many people continue to die each year from famines, and that many millions more go on perishing from persistent deprivation on a regular basis, is a calamity to which the world has, somewhat incredibly, got coolly accustomed. It does not seem to engender the kind of shock and disquiet that might be reasonable to expect given the enormity of the tragedy. Indeed, the subject often generates either cynicism ("not a lot can be done about it") or complacent irresponsibility ("don't blame me — it is not a problem for which I am answerable").

Perhaps this is what one should expect with a resilient and continuing calamity of this kind. But it is not at all easy to see why we do not owe each other even the minimal amounts of positive sympathy and solidarity that would make it hard for us to cultivate irresponsible complacency. While we shall not wait for an answer to that ethical question, we must address the issue of cynical pessimism (i.e., the belief that "not a lot can be done"). *There is, in*

___

2. To sign the Micah Call please go to *www.micahchallenge.org.*

fact, little reason for presuming that the terrible problems of hunger and starvation in the world cannot be changed by human action.[3]

Experts around the world, from different disciplines and political viewpoints, are chiming in with the same insight: *human action could end poverty in our generation.* The economist Jeffrey Sachs calls not only to halve income poverty by 2015 but to eradicate it by 2025.[4] Can churches play a part? Ronald Sider writes, "If at this moment in history a few million generous Christians blessed with material abundance dare to join hands with the poor around the world, we will decisively influence the course of world history."[5]

Why? There are over 6 billion people on earth. *Two billion* people identify themselves as Christians. Christians make up nearly one-third of the population on this planet. We are people from all walks of life, all languages, all colors, all income levels. We include those who negotiate loans for countries, political leaders, retired people, broadcasters, artists, mothers, teachers, businesspeople, and so on. The potential for constructive change if we invest our minds, hands, hearts, and resources in meeting the MDGs and align our efforts with other groups, is tremendous.

Structure of this book

Structured to look at global poverty from different viewpoints, *What Can One Person Do?* can seem a bit dizzying at first, so let us explain its organization. The book is designed for private reading and reflection as well as for study groups and includes material that can be used in worship services. It addresses issues for readers in both the US and the UK.

The book conveys a lot of information, so it doesn't unroll seamlessly like the hand-carved scroll of a Stradivarius cello or the melody it creates. Why? Because you can't respond to the question *What Can One Person Do?* on just one instrument. You need human stories and statistics, analysis and poetry, questions for reflection and calls to action. In fact, you need a little band.

Here is a speedy tour of the "band" of instruments that are playing through this book:

---

3. Jean Drèze and Amartya Sen, *Hunger and Public Action* (Oxford: Clarendon Press, 1989), 276; emphasis added.

4. Jeffrey Sachs, *The End of Poverty: Economic Possibilities for Our Time* (London and New York: Penguin, 2005).

5. Ronald Sider, *Rich Christians in an Age of Hunger*, 20th anniversary revision (Nashville: W Publishing Group, 1997), 272.

• **The Human Story.** Each chapter opens with the story of a real person or persons, looking into their life and experience. These can also be read aloud. (*Cello*)

• **The Main Chapter.** The body of each chapter explores an intersection of Christian faith and poverty reduction. (*Clarinet*)

• **MDG Briefings.** Readers will receive up-to-date briefings on different aspects of poverty with information on why each is important, what the main issues are, and progress so far. (*Percussion*)

• **Reflections.** Throughout the book there are poems, quotations, and meditations for spiritual reflection. These can be used in worship services too. (*Piccolo*)

• **Questions for Discussion.** The questions provide an opportunity for individuals and groups to pause and digest the materials, drawing in their own experience and insights. (*Tuba*)

• **Action Points.** Action points give individuals or groups specific, high-impact ways to use their limited time and resources strategically and effectively to reduce poverty and suffering. (*Saxophone*)

You might sometimes be startled when you were following the melody of the clarinet and then the percussion launches into an exuberant solo in a statistical briefing section. Or you might be whizzing through a Bible study and then be carried by the piccolo into poetry and prayer. The tuba might interrupt to grunt a rather basic question from the bassline. Or the sax might step to the front of the stage and belt out a call for action that feels a bit intrusive — or inspiring. We hope that you enjoy the concert.

Beyond a Dollar a Day

What Are the MDGs?

Living on Less Than a Dollar a Day

One of the reasons we are so aware of global poverty is that shocking statistics are readily available. One disturbing statistic to those of us in affluent societies is that over one-sixth of the world's population lives on less than the equivalent of US$1 a day.

What is it like to live on less than a dollar a day? The answer will vary between people and places. It will mean something different to someone living in a city in Eastern Europe, a shantytown in Africa, or a village in the mountains of South America. What it will mean to all, however, is severe hardship and insecurity, constant worries about food, and a daily struggle to get by.

The journalist Solomon Omollo — reporting for BBC Africa Live! *— decided to listen to what living on less than a dollar a day was like. He interviewed Dominic Nkhata and his wife, Patricia, a Zambian couple in their twenties with a two-year-old daughter.*

Dominic works as a factory hand while Patricia is a housewife. The couple are also responsible for four orphans, the children of Dominic's deceased sisters. The family live in two rooms in one of Lusaka's poorer neighborhoods, a shantytown called Garden Compound, . . . and are typical of the millions of Africans who live on less than a dollar a day.

Dominic earns 525,000 kwacha a month as his gross pay. After tax and other deductions, he's left with only 300,000 kwacha — roughly $40 — to take home with him. Juggling this meager income then becomes Patricia's headache — Dominic just hands the money to her: "When I get that money I just get confused. I tell her, just make your budget, whatever you plan is all right with me," he says.

The first thing Patricia does is to pay the rent, which takes up almost all the money. "After paying the rent," she says, "I sometimes have only about 10,000 kwacha ($2) left. That money is only enough for one day. The next morning I have to go and borrow some food or money from my family." Patricia buys

her food at a local market stall. She spends half of her remaining money —
$1 — on lunch. For six people, she can only afford six teaspoons of rice, three
tomatoes, two tablespoons of cooking oil, two onions and some salt. It's hardly
a nutritious meal. The rest of the money will be spent on an equally meager
supper.

It is all the more important that Patricia and Dominic should have a good
diet, because it could actually help prolong their lives — like 2 million other
Zambians they are infected with the HIV virus. Buying drugs of any kind is out
of the question for Dominic and Patricia.

Patricia and Dominic's situation is not unique. In their neighborhood, almost
everyone buys their groceries on credit if they want to eat, and according to
Patricia, many families in Garden Compound eat once a day. That's all they
can afford. "We can't buy anything with that money," Patricia says. "The food,
clothing, school fees. We look after four orphans too, but we can only afford
for one of them, the boy, to go to school. The rest are at home." . . .

Before Christmas I asked Zambia's finance minister, Peter Ngandu Magande,
who is to blame for the poverty of so many of his countrymen. . . . He conceded
that privatization had brought some poverty, but felt we were making too
much of an issue of living on less than a dollar a day. "In most of our Zambian
communities, particularly in rural areas, people do not pay for water, lighting,
housing and energy, so it is true that many of them live on less than $1 a day.
But then how does this become a problem worth singing about all over the
world?"

Asked how he would manage on a dollar a day he said he would buy
two kilos of maize meal worth 2,400 kwacha and spend the balance on fish
or meat, salt, and soap for the day. Maybe he knows a cheaper market than
Patricia and Dominic!

He also said that some Zambians wanted to live beyond their means: "On
such a tight budget," he said, "I will not afford television, radio, beer, a car,
or a mobile phone, which in a Zambian environment should be considered
luxuries." Well, Dominic and his family do not have any of those. Having a
square meal every day would be luxury enough.

— *Solomon Omollo; reproduced by*
kind permission of the BBC World Service.

This book is about the tension between extreme poverty — which seems
overwhelming — and the unique possibility this generation has to reduce
it. It is a call, a prayer, a plea, for action.

"You will always have the poor with you," Jesus said (Matthew
26:11). *And* he taught his disciples to feed, to heal, to liberate, to serve.
To live with this tension — between recurring human suffering and our
consistent, emphatic duty to respond — is something Christians can learn

to do well. We can learn that it is okay to be moved to the marrow by shocking facts — that 1 percent of people on earth earn more than the poorest 50 percent combined, for example. We can learn that it is possible to feed, heal, liberate, and serve in more effective and radical ways than we ever have before. We can learn to work effectively and to fail gracefully. Vitally, when we turn on the news and hear a tragic story of a tsunami or genocide or drought or financial crisis, we can learn how to reach for God and keep our own faith strong and pray to find more "laborers" to respond to extreme poverty (see Luke 10:2).

Yes, one person can do a great deal to reduce extreme poverty. Concrete actions can be taken. Change will come, if the action is informed and timely. This chapter gives an informational briefing on poverty. It begins with people like the Nkhata family who live in extreme poverty and then it describes global trends. It goes on to explain the Millennium Declaration and Millennium Development Goals, which can be a catalyst and a gathering point for Christians as well as others. It closes by exploring further why action by Christians — individuals, families, groups, and churches — can be uniquely effective in our time.

Global poverty

There are now 6.4 billion human beings, fashioned in the image of our Creator. Of these children of God, one in seven of us are hungry. One in seven us of live in urban slums. One in six of us lack clean water to drink. Over one in three of us lack basic sanitation. Nearly half of us live on less than $2 a day. Poor people are created in the image of God, and often their lives are far more radiant and blessed than these numbers convey. But this does not justify extreme involuntary material poverty. Let us listen to a few people who understand poverty.

A prominent study in sixty countries tried to understand how the poor defined poverty.[1] Teams would go to a village or neighborhood gathering and ask who the majority considered poor. Then the team would sit with the poor people and ask whether *they* considered themselves to be poor. If the people said yes, then the team would ask, "And what is poverty?" They replied:

- *"Poverty is like living in jail, living under bondage, waiting to be free."* (a person in Jamaica)

- Poverty is *"to come home and see your children go hungry and not have anything to give them."* (parents in Brazil)

---

1. Deepa Narayan et al., *Can Anyone Hear Us?* World Bank (Oxford: Oxford University Press, 2000).

- *"If you don't have money today, your disease will lead you to your grave."* (a person in Ghana)

- *"If I die there is no one to marry off my youngest daughter. I do not know whether I will be able to get food tomorrow. I do not see any light of hope."* (a man in Bangladesh)

- *"We are like garbage that everyone wants to get rid of."* (a blind woman in Moldova)

- *"A normal person has ... some self-esteem, to take a holiday, read a book. While now — you work here or there all day in order to have something to eat, and at night you can't even exchange a couple of words like normal persons, you drop off asleep as if you were dead. It's as if you were dead while you were still alive."* (a middle-aged woman in Bulgaria)

There is good news. Over the past thirty years global poverty has greatly decreased. In this time, the average life expectancy of a human

---

A World without Walls

What do you think that the people quoted above feel like if they go to a store or relative's house where there is a television and watch American and European programs from Jamaica, Brazil, South Africa, Bangladesh, Moldova, or Bulgaria — or from Afghanistan, China, Sierra Leone, Egypt, Iraq, India, or elsewhere?

People around the world are watching. In Guatemala, a low-income rural family living in a hut may save up for a high-status television. Very poor relatives may come and visit and see pictures of sizzling steaks and city streets and the news. People see us — including people who wonder where their next meal will come from.

?? QUESTIONS FOR DISCUSSION

- How do *you* feel when you think about people watching our lifestyles on television?

- How do you think the people quoted above feel when they see opulent lifestyles?

being increased by eight years. Thirty years ago about half of the world was illiterate; today three-quarters of us can read. One hundred and twenty million fewer people live on less than $1 a day now than in 1990. We stand on the shoulders of generations of dedicated people in faith communities, governments, and private initiatives worldwide that have contributed to these advances. Truly, there is much to celebrate.

At the same time, what we may not know is that for many people things got worse in the 1990s. It is tempting to think that everything is improving — computers are faster; wireless connections are better; cars are safer; medicines are more advanced. But in 2003 a United Nations report found that "some 54 countries are poorer now than in 1990. In 21 [countries], a larger proportion of people are going hungry. In 14, more children are dying before age five. In 12, primary school enrollments are shrinking. In 34, life expectancy has fallen. Such reversals in survival were previously rare."[2]

What can we do? A lot. The prominent 2005 MDG report *Investing in Development: A Practical Plan to Achieve the Millennium Development Goals,* led by Jeffrey Sachs, opens with this paragraph — a clarion call for action:

> We have the opportunity in the coming decade to cut world poverty by half. Billions more people could enjoy the fruits of the global economy. Tens of millions of lives can be saved. The practical solutions exist. The political framework is established. And for the first time, the costs are utterly affordable. Whatever one's motivation for attacking the crisis of extreme poverty — human rights, religious values, security, fiscal prudence, ideology — the solutions are the same. All that is needed is action.[3]

What Can One Person Do? shares the conviction (after scrutiny of the evidence) that the power to reduce extreme poverty — perhaps for the first time in history — lies in our hands. We must learn to use that power.

This book takes its title from the wonderful Pontius Puddle cartoon that sees the world, as it were, from God's view. Millions and millions of people are concerned. They are, one by one, raising their isolated prayers to God, "What can one person do?" "What can one church do?" "What can one nation do?" Together these lonely prayers of despair raise a deafening roar. The cartoon implies an obvious response: what would

---

2. United Nations Development Program, *Human Development Report* (New York: Oxford University Press, 2003).

3. United Nations Development Program, *Investing in Development: A Practical Plan to Achieve the Millennium Development Goals* (London: Earthscan, 2005).

happen if all who prayed in despair because they were "just one person, one church, one nation" resolved to work together? It is a question some are already asking.

The MDGs

Many of us make New Year's resolutions. At the turn of each year we take stock of our lives and pledge to change things for the better. Anyone who has made such resolutions will know how difficult it can be to stick to them. Yet sometimes looking back we realize that — however imperfect our steps were and however fragile and unsteady our convictions felt to us at the time — we actually, by the grace of God, turned a corner.

The advent of a new millennium encouraged many people to make special resolutions. Of these, surely one of the most important was made in New York in September 2000 at the Millennium Summit — the largest-ever gathering of heads of state. At this summit, the leaders of 189 nations unanimously adopted a United Nations resolution called the Millennium Declaration.

The Millennium Declaration provides a new compact for international cooperation. World leaders committed to act, saying, "We will spare no effort to free our fellow men, women, and children from the abject and dehumanizing conditions of extreme poverty to which more than a billion of them are now subjected."

The Millennium Declaration includes a series of poverty-reduction goals, the Millennium Development Goals, which are to:[4]

1. Eradicate extreme poverty and hunger.

2. Achieve universal primary education.

3. Promote gender equality and empower women.

4. Reduce child mortality.

---

4. A useful summary of the MDGs is contained in the Tearfund magazine *Footsteps* 63 (June 2005).

5. Improve maternal health.

6. Combat HIV/AIDS, malaria, and other diseases.

7. Ensure environmental sustainability.

8. Develop a global partnership for development.

Underlying these goals are eighteen clearly defined targets and forty-nine indicators that are used to monitor progress. This list may look limited, and the targets complicated. And yet, despite their limitations the MDGs provide the most comprehensive, integrated, and widely supported approach to tackling global poverty ever achieved. This is important, because history has demonstrated that there is no easy fix to global poverty. Poverty reduction is a multidimensional phenomenon requiring a coordinated response of many individuals, communities, organizations, and nations.

Why me?

What do these lofty goals have to do with our day-to-day lives, with our family, our church, our town? How are these goals a concern for any one of us? Aren't they for governments and other big players? For legitimate reasons, many of us will *avoid* any suggestion that *we* can act to reduce global poverty. We feel too little, too small, too much "just one person." Perhaps we say things like these:

"*Leave it to the experts.* I do not feel qualified to contribute. And I also think that the church's expertise is not in poverty reduction, either. So we should leave this work to others."

"*We should focus on equally important problems in our backyard.* There is growing poverty in my country and in my neighborhood. No other country is planning to help us. So we should focus our attention locally — if everyone did that it would be fine."

"*It's not my vocation.* I am passionate about other things. My time and resources are limited. God has not given me the gifts to do this work. Clearly other people do have such gifts and interests — let them do it."

"*Poverty can't be solved.* There will always be people who need support. There are poor in all countries of the world. Poverty eradication is impossible."

These are legitimate concerns, but they do not excuse inactivity. First, these goals cannot be met without widespread public support — as diverse experts like Sen, Drèze, Sachs's teams, and others stress. Second, the poorest people cannot lift themselves from poverty, and the wealth we enjoy is partly because of a trade system that is "rigged" in our favor. Third, deeply rooted in the Christian tradition is the imperative for each and every person of faith to care for the poor in whatever way they can — even if their primary vocation lies elsewhere. Finally, although relative poverty will always exist, and vulnerable people will always need extra support, extreme poverty, hunger, destitution, premature mortality, and illiteracy can all be drastically reduced using current knowledge. There is no other problem that causes such extensive suffering where the potential to overcome it lies so close at hand. The blockage to progress is not technical constraints; *it is a lack of political will and action.*

Beyond these reasons there is one more, and it has to do with the coherence between our faith and our own lives. Bryant Myers, a vice president of World Vision, writes, "I understand Christian witness to include the declaration of the gospel by life.... By *life* I refer to the fact that Christians are the message. We are the sixty-seventh book of the Bible. People read our lives, our actions and our words and believe they know what being a Christian means."[5]

Why are the MDGs strategic?

More people might act if they realize that the MDGs are different from previous poverty campaigns and are more realistic. Many promises have been made — and broken. Learning from these broken promises, the MDGs display four characteristics needed to foster change: consensus, collaboration, feasibility, and sustained attention. These characteristics, although set out for cooperation between nations, are just as important for local action and commitment. They are just as important for those in the pews as for presidents.

First, the MDGs have been publicly agreed upon by many different institutions and governments, so there is **consensus** on their vital importance and on the responses that would work. Some think that achieving the MDGs is important for reasons of global security and stability; others have personal or professional interests in furthering the MDGs; others think the MDGs are ethical imperatives. For many different reasons, diverse groups agree that we really must act to meet the MDGs.

---

5. Bryant L. Myers, *Walking with the Poor: Principles and Practices of Transformational Development* (Maryknoll, N.Y.: Orbis Books, 1999), 4.

View from Afar

Some people know little about the outside world. Some think that America and Europe are Christian civilizations. Some think that the streets of New York and London are paved with gold. Some impoverished Christians wonder whether Christians in rich countries know they exist. Christianity is not always evident from afar.

Wouldn't it be disappointing if Christians *do not* take a leading role among those who labor for a compassionate and durable response to extreme poverty? Wouldn't it seem natural that we *do*?

?? QUESTIONS FOR DISCUSSION

- What kind of witness can one person give to Christians and people of other faiths in other countries?
- What evidence does your church give of being compassionate and self-giving?

Second, the MDGs provide an unprecedented possibility for **collaboration**. Awareness about the MDGs and support for them are growing, not shrinking — nation by nation, community by community, person by person. The MDGs are a way to join with others and accomplish something together that we could not accomplish alone.

Third, the MDGs are **possible to achieve**. Of course it is hard to figure out what *is* feasible at a global level because so much is unknown and because experts disagree. Yet the research underlying the MDGs cuts across ideological lines and finds common ground. Leaders have attempted to choose goals that are regarded — perhaps for the first time in history — as feasible from many political and economic vantage points.

One reason the MDGs are possible to achieve is that they are **holistic**. The different goals address interconnected problems. For example, low levels of girls' education lead to higher infant mortality rates, greater hunger, and lower income. The MDGs therefore focus on a nexus of interconnected problems and address them together, rather than trying to address each one individually — because it is more difficult and costly to address them one by one than together.

Fourth, in comparison with most political planning, the MDGs have a relatively **long time horizon**. The goals are intended to break the "fad" mentality, in which one priority achieves great attention for a short period and then passes out of fashion before the task is finished. The problem is that a "short-term" mentality now plagues development initiatives which often demand results within one or two years, thus failing to bring about long-term structural changes, enduring solutions, and the cultivation of a different mentality. The difficulty, of course, is maintaining the momentum, interest, enthusiasm, and commitment for years to come. And so the campaign will need constant refreshing and reinvigoration.

The response so far

It is now 2005. Five years of the fifteen years set to achieve the MDGs have passed. Where are we? Well, trying to keep our promise and meet our resolution. Like many who make resolutions, we are progressing with shaky steps, uncertain if we will make it. The good news is that during the 1990s, China — which accounts for more than one-sixth of the world's population — lifted over 150 million people above $1 a day in income (Goal 1), an accomplishment worth celebrating. However, we need to reduce the proportion of income poor in other countries as well.

But there's another plot unfolding within this story. Awareness about the MDGs and the imperative to address global poverty is rising. In 2004 US and UK overseas development assistance (ODA) rose — only a bit, but it rose. In 2004, when the UK's chancellor of the exchequer, Gordon Brown, reported that we were not on track to meet the MDGs, he said, "If we let things slip, the millennium goals will become just another dream we once had, and we will indeed be sitting back on our sofas and switching on our TVs and, I am afraid, watching people die on our screens for the rest of our lives. We will be the generation that betrayed its own heart."[6] In 2005 the MDGs are regularly making the news, even in the popular press — and must continue to do so. As the 2005 report that monitors annual progress on the MDGs put it, "2005 is a crucial year to build momentum."[7]

---

6. Speech by the chancellor of the exchequer, Gordon Brown, at a conference titled "Making Globalization Work for All — The Challenge of Delivering the Monterrey Consensus" (February 16, 2004). Full text at *www.hm-treasury.gov.uk/newsroom_and_speeches/press/2004/press_12_04.cfm.*
7. *Millennium Development Goals: From Consensus to Momentum,* Global Monitoring Report (Washington, D.C.: World Bank, 2005).

We need such awareness. This book will give many examples of what we can do and what difference it would make if we did these things together. Let's take just one of those now — which is giving. Since 1970, the international community has asked the developed nations to give 0.7 percent of their gross national income (GNI) for development assistance — and at present five do. Goal 8 of the MDGs renews the 0.7 percent request. Why?

Well, the United States — by far the world's biggest economy (and one with a high proportion of self-identified Christians) — dedicates not 0.7 percent, not 0.5 percent, not 0.3 percent, not even 0.2 percent, but only 0.16 percent of its gross national income to development assistance (and not all of that is related to poverty). This is less than 1 *percent* of the government's budget. People's private giving is also low — less than 2 percent of private giving goes overseas (see Action 3). The UK government gives 0.36 percent. The world's rich countries today give *half* as much, as a proportion of their income, as they did in the 1960s.

Most people think that their countries are far more generous than this. In fact, year after year public opinion polls show that we think that the governments give *much* more than they do.

What can we do, as people of faith? As Action 3 suggests, we can set an example and give at least 0.7 percent of our own income to reduce extreme poverty in developing countries, then take action so that our friends and churches and, eventually, our countries do likewise.

Despite the slow progress initially, the MDGs are awakening many people from different professional, religious, national, artistic, and other backgrounds to their responsibility (and ability) to care for the poor — from Bono to Nelson Mandela. They provide a common language in which to talk about poverty and work together to address it. It would be very easy for us to let this opportunity to work together pass and go back to our individual prayers of concerned despair and to think we were daft for making the resolution in the first place. Yet it is also possible for churches to play a significant role in sustaining the momentum and affecting the process so that we turn the corner.

Could it work?

Yes — honestly, it could. Even given the permanent fallibilities of human nature, it could. For we have gotten better at reducing poverty. This is important information, given not only the increases in poverty during the 1990s but also the well-known failures associated with ODA and development programs. Mistakes include development programs that were wasted; or that propped up corruption, patriarchy, or racism; or funded unproductive investments such as dams that did not work and factories that were not maintained. It includes bad policies such as closing functioning schools and health clinics to save money to repay debts, and ignoring the HIV/AIDS pandemic for too long. Although some of these mistakes recur, many development agencies, NGOs, governments, and civil society groups now work differently. In particular, they have identified the following as significant advances:

+ Investing ODA in poverty reduction and not "tying" it to donors' expensive products.

+ Abandoning large-scale poverty reduction projects that don't work.

+ Recognizing the importance of good governance and accountability and of preventing corruption.

+ Promoting pro-poor growth (economic growth where the poor obtain jobs and increase their income).

+ Putting resources in the hands of the poor through micro-credit and community-driven development.

+ Involving the poor to build their skills and empower them to lead activities in their area.

+ Improving education and health systems.

+ Collecting social and economic data regularly to track progress and underpin policy.

+ Advancing technology related to heath care, agriculture, communications, and so on.

This chapter has provided some basic information on poverty and introduced the MDGs as a set of tasks we might put our hands to. Subsequent chapters will move on to consider both faith and effectiveness: faith, because Christians who act to reduce poverty might be responding to a moral and spiritual call that lies at the root of our faith. It is simultaneously apparent that if enough people turned their love and energy to this particular set of tasks we might also be effective, overturning the stifling and demotivating belief that "not a lot can be done" and demonstrating what can be done to reduce extreme poverty.

MDGs

Goal 8: Develop a global partnership for development

In each chapter, we'll include a "briefing" section like this one, to introduce you to a goal. These sections provide the "percussion" mentioned in
the introduction.

There are eight MDGs, and we start with the last one. Why? Because it alone
addresses the UK, the US, and other wealthy countries. It describes what we
can do to catalyze and support the MDGs. It primarily addresses our need to:

* Increase overseas development assistance and improve what we give. (*Aid*)

* Change unjust trade policies. (*Trade*)

* Support all countries in moving to sustainable debt burdens. (*Debt Relief*)

The goal also includes targets related to technology transfers, affordable
essential drugs, youth employment, and special needs of certain countries.

More and Better Aid: With respect to aid (termed overseas development
assistance, or ODA), the goals are to increase net ODA; to increase the proportion of ODA that addresses poverty reduction and basic social services; to
allocate ODA strategically, favoring poorer and disadvantaged countries; and
to make sure that the ODA is untied — which means that countries do not
have to buy expensive products from the rich donor countries when similar
products are available at a fraction of the cost from elsewhere. As the chart
on page 36 shows, our total ODA together — tied and untied — has not kept
pace with the wealth we have enjoyed from economic growth.

Trade: With respect to trade, the aims are to increase imports from developing countries, to decrease tariffs on agricultural products and textiles in rich
countries, to decrease domestic subsidies in rich countries for their own agricultural industries, and to provide financial assistance to developing countries
to increase their trade capacity.

Debt Relief: With respect to debt relief, this MDG stresses the need to
make sure that the highly indebted poor countries have advanced to the point
that they can — and do — receive debt relief that is in turn invested in poverty
reduction. They must also put into place adequate measures to prevent future
debt crises.

0.7 percent: A benchmark for giving

Since 1970, the international community has asked the developed nations to
give 0.7 percent of their gross national income (GNI) for development assistance. This figure was chosen after careful calculations to determine what level
of financial giving would make a significant contribution to poverty reduction.
It was reaffirmed in 2002 at a meeting in Monterrey. At present only five out of

twenty-four developed nations give 0.7 percent or more: Norway, Denmark, the Netherlands, Luxembourg, and Sweden. Six countries have announced timetables to meet the 0.7 percent goal: Belgium, Finland, France, Ireland, Spain, and the UK. Goal 8 of the MDGs renews the 0.7 percent request for all donor countries and asks developing nations to give 0.15 percent of their GNI.

The good news is that ODA has increased recently from a historic low of 0.22 percent in 1997. In 2003, which is the last year for which there are firm figures, ODA averaged 0.25 percent of GNI, or $60 billion in 2001 dollars. It is estimated to have increased by 5 percent, or $3 billion in constant prices, in 2004.

2004 Overseas Development Assistance as Percentage of Gross National Income

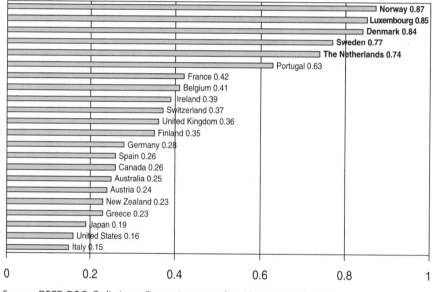

Source: OECD DAC, *Preliminary Figures* (*www.oecd.org/dac*; accessed 2005).

ACTION I:
THE POWER OF PRAYER

The American theologian Walter Wink has written, "History belongs to the intercessors, who believe the future into being."[8] This action asks you to become an intercessor on behalf of the poor and those who work to address poverty. Prayer is the way that we join our work with God's work, our hope with God's hope. It is the way we connect our actions and love with the mission of God, and the way that we are spiritually renewed. When we are grounded in prayer, God can use us.

As chapter 8 also describes, there are many ways to pray. One way is to enjoy the silence of contemplative prayer in which one stills the heart and mind in the presence of God. Another is to exercise the imagination in a meditative engagement with scripture. There are prayers of praise and adoration through songs or psalms. There are prayers of penance. Some prayers seek comfort or healing or strength, while others dedicate a day or an event or a meeting to God and ask God's presence in it. Some prayers are more like a running conversation. There are also the "arrow prayers," in which the mind shoots up to God while a Web site is loading or while waiting for a traffic light to change. Many are the ways that Christians enter into dialogue with God, and prayer can be described most simply as conversation with God.

Prayer is more than speaking the words, for to pray with the lips when the heart does not lean toward God has been viewed as a temptation by many. Intercessory prayer is earnest prayer on another's behalf. In intercessory prayer we draw other people into God's presence and ask God's blessing upon them. In chapter 8 we mention a nun who, upon listening to the daily news, draws the stories into the "crossing point" between the pain we inflict upon one another — by design and by irresponsible neglect and by default — and the love of God, which can overcome all darkness. Intercessory prayer invites us to extend our compassion beyond ourselves and our families to the wider community and to strangers both poor and powerful.

Why is prayer strategic?

We do not know how prayer "works" or exercises influence in the external world. It certainly does not stop all wars, or prevent all genocides, or end global poverty overnight. Experimental double-blind psychological

---

8. Walter Wink, *Engaging the Powers: Discernment and Resistance in a World of Domination* (Minneapolis: Fortress Press, 1992), 299.

studies of healing prayer suggest that people who are prayed for fare better than those who are not. Furthermore, those who pray consistently and deeply, and those who are prayed for, often have tremendously powerful stories to tell. But there is much we do not understand, and people's views about the power of prayer differ considerably.

What is clear is that one of the paths by which God works is in the heart of the individual or community that prays. As Robert Llewellyn, the former chaplain at the shrine of Julian of Norwich, wrote, "We do not go to prayer that we may use God but that he may use us. We trust him to use our prayer as he wills in the extension of his blessing. And we trust him further to make us, through the discipline and training of prayer, more effective instruments of his will.... And prayer for one another will build us up into a fellowship of love, the deepest of all blessings, from which much else will flow."[9] John of the Cross, a mystic and church reformer in the sixteenth century, was really quite direct in his advocacy of prayer:

> Those who are very active and think that they are going to encircle the earth with their preaching... should realise that they would do the Church much more good, and please God much more... if they spent even half of this time being with God in prayer.... In this way they would certainly achieve more with less trouble in one work than they would have done in a thousand. (*Canticle* 29:3)

Spiritual renewal is our basic aim even when we consider the exigencies of destitution, because by such renewal God will be able to use us more fully for many purposes, including confronting extreme poverty. If the 2 billion Christians each do our bit — even if imperfectly and incompletely and somewhat inconsistently — faithfulness will be felt. But there cannot be spiritual renewal without a deepening life of prayer. One kind of prayer that seems to flow naturally is prayer that holds economic issues, the concerns of the poor, and the work of those who seek to serve them, before God.

How to intercede

Here is a practical way to start to pray for others: purchase a postcard. Then read the newspaper, or the newsletter or Web site of an organization you are giving to, or your church's partners and the organizations it supports. Write the names of people or organizations or situations on

---

9. Robert Llewellyn, *Prayer and Contemplation* (London: Marshall Pickering, 1989), 21.

the postcard. If you write small and in two columns, up to forty names fit (of course some of these will also be your loved ones or colleagues). Then pick up the postcard and pray for those on your list one by one, holding each in your mind until the image is formed, holding them up to God, willing the wholeness of body, mind, heart, and soul, asking God's healing and loving-kindness and blessing to be with them. Keep the postcard in an accessible place and do this in spare moments. You won't get through every name every day, but the point is you will pray, and care, regularly. And, as you need to add names to your list that do not fit there, simply buy a new postcard and begin again.

Another option is to buy or download an international cycle of prayer and use it individually or in your church. Many churches have these, and they lift up a particular part of the church — and you might add the poor persons in the region of the church — every day. When a church prays regularly for others across the globe, it not only expresses potent prayers of the church and broadens the horizons of love for a church community, it is also an appealing witness of concern to visitors.

Sometimes it seems that prayer takes too much time, and we do not believe we have the time. But prayer is really just an attitude of being attuned to God. As Martin Luther wrote:

> There is no Christian who does not have time to pray without ceasing. But I mean the spiritual praying, that is: no one is so heavily burdened with his labor, but that if he will he can, while working, speak with God in his heart, lay before Him his need and that of other men, ask for help, make petition, and in all this exercise and strengthen his faith.[10]

However busy we are, there are moments into which we can slip prayer. If nothing else, while we listen to the news we can spend just a few seconds lifting up the people involved in the stories we hear.

We close with four prayers that you might find helpful. One is from the second century, one by young people in Kenya, one is a prayer for the churches, and the last is a grace from South America that can be said at mealtimes.

---

10. Martin Luther, *Treatise on Good Works*, part 2.7.

Prayers

We beg you, Lord, to help and defend us. Deliver the oppressed, pity the insignificant, raise the fallen, show yourself to the needy, heal the sick, bring back those who have gone astray, feed the hungry, lift up the weak, take off the prisoners' chains. May every nation come to know that you alone are God, that Jesus Christ is your Child, that we are your people, the sheep that you pasture. Amen.

— Clement of Rome, circa AD 100

We pray for people
so poor
that they cannot help themselves;
whose subsistence crops
have been destroyed by climatic disasters;
for people who live in areas
where rainfall is unreliable
and varies from year to year.
We pray for small children
who die of malnutrition,
and others who suffer from disease
because their mothers do not understand
the values of different kinds of foods.
We pray for little children,
too young
to pray for themselves.

— Written by young people in Kenya[11]

11. Angela Ashwin, *The Book of a Thousand Prayers* (London: Marshall Pickering, 1996), 168.

Most loving God,
as your desire for mercy for the poor is unrelenting,
may we be unrelenting in our pursuit of mercy for all;
as your compassion for the suffering of the poor knows no limit,
may our hearts overflow with compassion for all;
as you long for justice for the poor,
may we strive for justice for all.
Open our eyes to the structures of oppression from which we benefit,
and give us courage to accept our responsibility,
wisdom to chart a sound course amid complexity,
and perseverance to continue our work until it is finished.
Breathe your life-giving Spirit afresh into your Church
to free us from apathy and indifference;
through Jesus Christ our Lord.
Amen.

—Episcopalians for Global Reconciliation

Give bread to those who are hungry;
give hunger for justice to those who have bread. Amen.

—South American table grace

2

The Mission of God

Urban Poverty in the Philippines

For the first time in human history, the majority of the world's people live in towns and cities. An increasing proportion of the world's poor are the urban poor. In Cebu City in the Philippines 69 percent of the population are squatters, without any rights to the land they live on. Glitzy shopping centers contrast starkly with appalling squatter communities that often lack the most basic of services. Although most poor people have been living where they are for decades, new developments mean many are now threatened by evictions. In at least one situation, however, eviction provided an opportunity for the squatters to learn how to organize and create a new community.

Mary Ann Ferraren is president of a squatters' residents association in Cebu City. She describes below her experience working with an NGO called FORGE to lobby local governments for basic services, security of tenure, and new land on which to build permanent homes. FORGE receives financial and other assistance from Christian Aid, their UK development partner.

We received notice of eviction on January 24, 2001. We had many anxieties. We were relocated in April 2001. We had nothing at first. No light, no water, no roads. We had nothing but the materials we had from demolishing our homes. We met Gwen of FORGE in March 2002. She introduced us to Vidal, our community organizer, who introduced us to an NGO that helped us fix up a water supply. By May, we had water.

Since we were a new organization and we'd all been uprooted, we were all rebuilding our houses, so we were a bit disorganized. But Vidal kept coming to the meetings and guiding us. He helped us set up financial systems and tap people for help. After six months of following up with a private electric company, we got electricity.

As president, I attend seminars at FORGE to help me lead better and play my role better. I've had training...and a course in financial management. As you know, if you don't know how to manage your money properly, suddenly there's no money. Now, we're involved in livelihood project management. That is what I enjoy most.

42

... These houses are our very own, and we'll improve them over time. We'll get cement floors, and more walls. We are 55 families with children of all ages, and we have one water supply. But we are lucky to have it....

If we were people of little faith, we would not be able to build our houses here. There was nothing but a dry riverbed. Without faith, how could we see it as home? Uprooting is very difficult for people.

In June, we do Novena (nine days of prayers) in honor of our patron saint, Mary, Mother of Perpetual Help. If we did not believe in the merciful and loving Father, our children would not be happy like these children are. We've been here only one year and three months, and already we will soon have our own chapel. We are nothing without Him.

Thanks too to the friends in the UK. I know that even if they are rich, when they make a donation, they sacrifice a pound of meat, no?

*— This adapted account is included
by kind permission of Christian Aid.*

The question *What can one person do?* begins, appropriately enough, with the individual person, his or her agency and action. In light of the facts and figures that we have just outlined, the caring person, the committed Christian, hopefully is now asking, "What can one person do in a world of such crushing widespread poverty?" Or perhaps, if we are really honest with ourselves, we might now even be risking the question, "What can *I* do to address the suffering of the poor in the world?" These are good and important questions, and we do not want to lose the focus on individual agency and personal responsibility in overcoming poverty. As Christians we do believe that each and every person is created in the image and likeness of God. We believe that God loves each and every one of us in all of our uniqueness and has given gifts that can be used to glorify God and God's creation. We therefore do not want to downplay the individual and his or her role in combating global poverty. But at this point we want to pause and move the focus from the individual to God. We want to ask, what it is that God is doing in this world? What is it that God wills for creation? Once we have this big picture of what God wants, then we can more productively and creatively understand what our role is in God's project, God's mission for the world.

As Christians we are never autonomous individuals, living and functioning separate from our communities of faith. It is impossible, or at least very difficult, to be a Christian all by oneself. Even a monastic individual living a solitary life is connected to the community of faith through prayer and intercessions. Any discussion of what God is up to in the lives of Christians must be grounded in a specific context of belief and practice. The necessity of grounding belief and practice within a specific church context is important to our discussion at this point because as we move into a study of God's mission we will approach it from the perspective of one particular church community, the Episcopal Church in the United States. This is not to privilege the Episcopal Church over other churches or theological and ecclesial perspectives. Rather, starting from one faith community (namely, the Episcopal Church) offers an incarnational, contextual glimpse into how a Christian community engages God's mission.

The reader is thus invited to use the "case study" of the Episcopal Church as a point of departure, a point of comparison, for understanding what God is doing in his or her life and faith community. We all must start somewhere, in some specific context, when we consider what we can do to address global poverty. How does the case of the Episcopal Church's engagement with God's mission, offered here, draw us even more deeply into the question *What can one person do?* Or perhaps the more specific question at hand is, What can I do from within my faith community to address global poverty?

The biblical call to God's mission

The great African American biblical scholar Verna Dozier once said, "Christians should be able to tell the whole biblical story in one sitting." Dr. Dozier was a skilled and accomplished storyteller. Multitudes of students have sat spellbound at her feet as she broke open the books of the Bible, weaving them into an integrated story of what God is doing in the world. In her telling, the Bible has a common thread that runs from Genesis to Revelation. And that thread is that God loves the world and all that is in it, and God seeks to make all things new and whole. For missiologists (scholars of the history and theology of Christian mission) the love of God for the world and the desire of God to make all things new is understood as God's mission, God's purpose, in the world. Thus for Dozier, and for all engaged in mission, it is imperative that we see the Bible as an integrated whole with a clear and unified message. And that message has everything to do with the mission of God, which is known in Latin as the *missio Dei.*

So what does holy scripture say about mission? Oddly, the word "mission" is not found in the Bible. Yes, the seventy are sent out, and there are various references in St. Paul's epistles to sending, but mission as it has been historically understood — as the sending of specific individuals to faraway places to convert others — is glaringly absent. Maybe the reason that we do not find the word "mission" in the Bible is because *all* of holy scripture is the story of mission, God's mission. The whole Bible, the Hebrew scriptures and the New Testament, is a revelation of God's mission in the world. Notice that the Bible, we argue, reveals God's mission — not the church's mission, or your mission, or my mission. For ultimately it is God's mission that our Lord Jesus came to bear witness to, it is God's mission that the church proclaims in the world today, and it is God's mission that we share in by virtue of our baptism. So what is God's mission?

In the opening chapter of Genesis we learn that God is the God of all creation. Out of God's love, God brought everything into being, the heavens, the earth, all living creatures including humanity, and "it was good." At the very start of the biblical story we learn that God is a God of the whole cosmos, a universal God, who watches over and cares for all of creation. The story continues, however. No sooner had this universal, loving God created humankind than we turned our backs on God. We chose to live unto ourselves. We became alienated from the love and power of God, and we became alienated from each other, and our relationships became distorted. Sin is less about actions and more about a state of separation, separation from God, separation from each other, separation from all creation. Sin is about isolation, division, and broken relationships.

But God does not want humans to be alienated from God and from each other. The loving Creator chooses to rebuild the bonds of love that are severed through human sin. God's mission is to reconnect with humanity and heal the divisions that separate us. The central element of God's mission, the *missio Dei,* is God's commitment to restore to unity that which had become broken, to reconcile a divided world, to heal a hurting humanity.

To fulfill this mission God chose a particular people as an entry point into the world. Through Abraham and Sarah and their descendants, God began a new relationship with humankind. God says to Abraham:

> Behold, my covenant is with you, . . . and you shall be the father of a multitude of nations. . . . I will make you exceedingly fruitful; and I will make nations of you, and kings shall come forth from you. And I will establish my covenant between me and you and your descendants after you throughout their generations for an everlasting covenant, to be God to you and to your descendants after you. And I will give to you, and to your descendants after you, the land of your sojournings, all the land of Canaan, for an everlasting possession; and I will be their God. (Genesis 17:2–8)

The whole of Hebrew scripture is the telling and retelling of the quest for relationship between God and God's chosen people.

To help define this relationship God gave the Law. The Law stood as God's assurance of God's love and faithfulness. In Exodus God promises Moses and his people:

> If you will obey my voice and keep my covenant, you shall be my own possession among all peoples; for all the earth is mine, and you shall be to me a kingdom of priests and a holy nation.
>
> (Exodus 19:5–6)

The Law stood as God's assurance of love and faithfulness. In the giving of the Law, God sought to establish Israel as the leadership of a new world order. By following God's commandments the chosen people would stand as a beacon of hope in a world separated from God.

God's covenant with the Jews was not, however, an exclusive arrangement. The new relationship begun with Abraham, and clarified by the Law, was intended for all of humanity. God's covenant was to be the vehicle, the door, by which all the peoples of the world could be joined both to the almighty Creator and to each other. Israel was to serve as a centripetal force pulling all of humanity back into relationship with God.[1] Abraham and Sarah's descendants thus were to be agents of reconciliation between God and an errant humanity. All the nations were to come to God through the covenant. The prophets, especially the servant songs of Isaiah, testify to this calling. In Isaiah 42 God says to his chosen people:

> I am the Lord, I have called you in righteousness, I have taken you by the hand and kept you; I have given you as a covenant to the people, a light to the nations, to open the eyes that are blind, to bring out the prisoners from the dungeon, from the prison those who sit in darkness. (Isaiah 42:6–7)

And again in Isaiah 49:

> It is too light a thing that you should be my servant to raise up the tribes of Jacob and to restore the preserved of Israel; I will give you as a light to the nations, that my salvation may reach to the end of the earth. (Isaiah 49:6)

---

1. See Johannes Blauw, *The Missionary Nature of the Church* (New York: McGraw-Hill, 1962), and Donald Senior and Carroll Stuhlmueller, *The Biblical Foundations for Mission* (Maryknoll, N.Y.: Orbis Books, 1984).

The servant songs of Isaiah proclaim clearly that God's mission in the world is to bring salvation to the ends of the earth; to set free those who are oppressed; to open the eyes of the blind (Isaiah 42:6–7); to heal the separation between God, humanity, and all of creation; to restore to unity with God all the peoples of the world and all of creation. In Isaiah we find the affirmation of Israel's commission, or co-mission, with God.

The story of God's mission, however, does not end with Abraham's covenant. It goes on. As Christians we affirm that because of God's love for the world and desire to be united with all of humanity, God took one final decisive step. In the incarnation of Jesus Christ, God enters the world anew and takes the responsibility for God's mission directly upon himself:

> For God so loved the world that he gave his only Son, that whoever believes in him should not perish but have eternal life. God sent the Son into the world not to condemn the world, but that the world might be saved through him. (John 3:16–17).

In Jesus, God creates a new covenant, a new means by which all the world could be joined to the Creator. Jesus was sent into the world to be the way, the truth, and the life (John 14:6). As the human form of the creator God, Jesus' mission is coterminous, one and the same, with that of the Creator. His mission is God's mission.

The ultimate act of Jesus' self-giving participation in God's mission is his sacrifice upon the cross and victory over death. The joining of Jesus' pain and suffering on the cross with our pain and suffering where we are passionately connected with God, with one other, and with all creation. On the cross is where this new relationship, this right relationship, with God and each other is effected. In Jesus' resurrection we are given the promise of restored life in him. This is what we mean by Jesus' atonement: his atonement is our at-one-ment, our at-one-ment with God and our at-one-ment with each other. In Jesus' death and resurrection we are given the means by which we become one with each other and with God. In the death and resurrection of Jesus the divisions between God and humanity are overcome, and the promise of reconciliation is made real.

The reality that Jesus takes on God's mission in his incarnation, death, and resurrection is not a departure from the mission that God entrusted to Israel. Jesus did not come to break down the Law but to fulfill it. Jesus testifies to his fulfillment of the Isaiah prophesy in Luke's Gospel:

The Spirit of the Lord is upon me, because he has anointed me to preach good news to the poor. He has sent me to proclaim release to the captives and recovering of sight to the blind, to set at liberty those who are oppressed, to proclaim the acceptable year of the Lord. (Luke 4:18–19)

Over and over again, Jesus demonstrates his solidarity with, and preferential option for, the poor, the sick, the outcasts, and those at the periphery of society, like the urban poor in Cebu City. The Gospels are a living testimony to Jesus' life and ministry as the source of God's salvation for the world. In Jesus the reign of God is made real and tangible in our broken world.

Although Jesus is the fulfillment of the Law and prophets, there is, however, a difference between God's mission as it was entrusted to the Jews and how it was realized in Jesus the Christ. Whereas Israel represented a calling-in of humanity to union with God, Jesus turned the direction of God's mission around. Instead of a centripetal force, God's mission, realized in Jesus and empowered by the Holy Spirit, becomes a centrifugal force, a going out. Jesus demonstrates in word and deed that the reign of God, made real in the sending of God's Son, must continue to expand, to move out to the ends of the earth. "As you have sent me into the world, so I have sent them into the world" (John 17:18). Jesus thus sends out his disciples, empowered by the Holy Spirit, to be the bearers of his mission, God's mission, in the world.

And Jesus called to him the twelve and began to send them out two by two and gave them authority over unclean spirits....So they went out and preached that people should repent. And they cast out many demons, and anointed with oil many that were sick and healed them. (Mark 6:7, 12–13)

And to the seventy Jesus said:

Go your way; Whenever you enter a town and they receive you, eat what is set before you; heal the sick in it and say to them, "The Kingdom of God has come near to you." (Luke 10:3, 8–9)

Notice here that God's mission, fulfilled in the incarnation of Jesus and then furthered by the sending-out of the disciples in the power of the Spirit, is multiform. There is loving service, feeding the hungry, healing the sick, and setting free the oppressed. But these acts of love are always coupled with the proclamation of the kingdom of heaven. In other words, God's mission to unite all of humanity to one another and to God is realized through acts of love and justice combined with the proclamation of Jesus as the Christ, the Savior of the world. The wholeness of God's mission is discovered in the combination of Jesus' "new commandment" — "Just as I have loved you, so you also should love one another" (John 13:34) — with the Great Commission, to make disciples of all nations, baptizing them in the name of the Father and the Son and the Holy Spirit (Matthew 28:19).

The movement of God's mission in heralding and making real the reign of God to the ends of the earth is exemplified in the life and writings of Paul. We cannot develop here the complete mission theology of Paul, but we do want to highlight two fundamental aspects of Paul's own role in God's mission. The first is that Paul and his coworkers reached out to the Gentiles with the good news of Jesus Christ. It is true that in the Gospels we are given evidence of Jesus' mission to the Gentiles: see, for example, our Lord's healing of the centurion's slave (Luke 7:1–10) and his curing of the Canaanite woman's daughter (Matthew 15:21–28). But it is in the life and ministry of Paul that God's mission expands beyond Palestine. The second thing we want to emphasize about Paul's mission theology is the full development of the church as the body of Christ in the world today. In the Letter to the Ephesians (probably written by one of Paul's disciples) we find testimony that all who follow Jesus Christ, Jew and Gentile alike, are united with God the Creator:

> And Jesus came and preached peace to you who were far off and peace to those who were near; for through him we both have access in one Spirit to the Father. So then you are no longer strangers and sojourners, but you are fellow citizens with the saints and members of the household of God, built upon the foundation of the apostles and prophets, Christ Jesus himself being the cornerstone, in whom the whole structure is joined together and grows into a holy temple of the Lord; in whom you also are built into it for a dwelling place of God in the Spirit. (Ephesians 2:17–22)

As followers of Jesus Christ today, as the church, we too share in this household of God and thus are called to preach peace to those who are far off and to those who are near. Participation in God's mission, therefore, is at the heart of the baptismal call. Baptism is our commission, co-mission, in God's mission. Just as God sent Jesus into the world, and Jesus sent his disciples to the ends of the earth, we too are sent in mission.

In the "catechism" in the Episcopalian Book of Common Prayer we find a profound missiological affirmation of the relationship between the church and God's mission. This catechism states, "The mission of the Church is to restore all people to unity with God and each other in Christ."[2] The calling of the church, the calling of every Christian of any denomination, is to participate with God in the restoration of unity between ourselves and God and ourselves and each other — to participate in the *missio Dei.* It is the work of the church to herald and effect the new order where alienation, division, and separation give way to inclusion, reconciliation, and unity. As the body of Christ in the world today, we are called to work for the restoration to unity of all people with God and each other in Christ. The eminent missiologist David Bosch has summarized it thus:

> Mission is, primarily and ultimately, the work of the Triune God, Creator, Redeemer, and Sanctifier, for the sake of the world, a ministry in which the church is privileged to participate. This is the deepest source of mission.... There is mission because God loves people.[3]

Our identity as followers of Christ is dependent upon, and judged against, how faithful we are to the mission of God, to the making real of God's reconciling love in the world. As Christians, we are called to live beyond ourselves, trusting that God will use us to effect God's restoration to unity — God's redemption of creation to wholeness and oneness in Christ.

From "missions" to God's mission

This chapter seeks to encourage faithful Christians to participate in the mission of God. We have posited that a complete reading of the biblical story tells of a God whose purpose it is — whose mission it is — to preach good news to the poor, to heal, reconcile, and restore a broken and hurting world. A good question for us now to turn to is, What lessons can we learn from the history of Christian missions?[4]

In the not-too-distant past the conversion of "the heathen," the spread of churches, and the advance of Western "civilization" went hand in hand. The abuses, as well as the contributions, of missionaries and the close connection between mission and imperialism in Africa, Asia,

---

2. Book of Common Prayer, 855.

3. David J. Bosch, *Transforming Mission: Paradigm Shifts in Theology of Mission* (Maryknoll, N.Y.: Orbis Books, 1991), 392.

4. Part of the following section has been previously published in Ian T. Douglas, "Baptized into Mission: Ministry and Holy Orders Reconsidered," *Sewanee Theological Review* 40, no. 4 (Michaelmas 1997): 431–43.

Latin America, and Oceania are well documented.[5] Throughout the nine-
teenth century and for the first half of the twentieth century the Western
churches had their missions. These missions, as dependent outposts of
European and North American Christianity, sought to extend church
models and cultural worldviews of the Enlightenment.

In the middle of the twentieth century, significant shifts in the theological terrain of an emergent global Christianity began to shake the model
of mission. Quakes occurred and fissures opened up between established
models of mission and new understandings of mission in the emerging
postcolonial, postmodern world. Mission was seen less as something
done by voluntary associations of Christians (often as a side interest of
the churches) and more as the central calling of the church. Such theological shifts led the theologian Emil Brunner to state, "The Church exists
by mission as fire exists by burning," and Stephen Neill to proclaim,
"The age of missions is at an end; the age of mission has begun."[6]

The church-centered view of mission was short-lived. Christians
swiftly began to look beyond the church for the locus of God's action in
the world. Increasingly the church was seen as adjunct to God's salvation work in the wider struggles of the world. The *missio ecclesia* (the
church's mission) was to give way to the *missio Dei* (the mission of God).

The church as the body of Christ in the world is called and empowered
by the Holy Spirit to participate with God in God's mission of reconciliation, redemption, and liberation. Although having a unique and central
role in God's plan of salvation, the church does not have exclusive rights
on participation with God in God's mission. Thus many think it possible
to cooperate with people of other faiths in God's universal mission. As
the southern Indian theologian S. J. Samartha puts it, "In a religiously
plural world, Christians, together with their neighbors of other faiths,
are called upon to participate in God's continuing mission in the world.
Mission is God's continuing activity through the Spirit to mend the brokenness of creation, to overcome the fragmentation of humanity, and to
heal the rift between humanity, nature and God."[7]

Our call to God's mission

In this chapter we have argued that the church's calling is to participate
with God in mending the brokenness of creation and healing the rift

5. For an overview of the Episcopal Church, USA and its foreign mission history, see
Ian T. Douglas, *Fling Out the Banner: The National Church Ideal and the Foreign Mission of
the Episcopal Church* (New York: Church Hymnal Corporation, 1996).

6. Stephen Neill, *A History of Christian Missions* (New York: Penguin Books, 1964), 572.

7. S. J. Samartha, *One Christ — Many Religions: Towards a Revised Christology*
(Maryknoll, N.Y.: Orbis Books, 1995), 149.

between humanity, nature, and God. Echoing the biblical story, the mission of God, the mission of Jesus, and the mission of the church is one of reconciliation and redemption. We have also argued that this mission has a distinct bias toward those who are impoverished and marginalized, as Jesus was sent by God "to bring good news to the poor, . . . to proclaim release to the captives and recovery of sight to the blind, to let the oppressed go free, to proclaim the year of the Lord's favor" (Luke 4:18–19). God's mission, manifested in Jesus and empowered by the Holy Spirit, is not static but a centrifugal force of movement outward. Jesus demonstrated in word and deed that the reign of God, realized in the sending of God's Son, must continue to expand to the ends of the earth. "As you have sent me into the world, so I have sent them into the world" (John 17:18). Jesus' disciples are sent to bear his mission, God's mission, in the world.

For over a century and a half the Episcopal Church has affirmed that baptism incorporates the faithful into the mission of God. The General Convention (the governing body of the Episcopal Church) proclaimed boldly in 1835 that the church was to be first and foremost a missionary society. All Episcopalians, by virtue of baptism and not voluntary association, were members of the Domestic and Foreign Missionary Society.[8] Participation in God's mission therefore is at the heart of the baptismal call. Baptism is thus a commission, co-mission, in God's mission. Just as God sent Jesus into the world, and Jesus sent his disciples to the ends of the earth, we too are sent in mission. The imperative is clear.

It is important to emphasize that the point of departure for participation in the *missio Dei* is baptism. Baptism, not ordination, is where the calling to a life of mission originates. The work of mission, the work of the church, belongs to the *laos,* as the people of God. Engaging with the MDGs is one practical expression of that mission — and there are others.

To conclude, the mark of mission is not defined by activity or geographic location or holy orders but rather by the process of crossing frontiers from the known to the unknown, from the safe to the dangerous, from the comfortable to the uncomfortable.

Mission involves risk. It means risking oneself, one's control, and ultimately one's faith. Discovering God anew in those who are radically

---

8. *Journal of the Proceedings of the Bishops, Clergy and Laity of the Protestant Episcopal Church in the United States of America in a General Convention 1835* (New York: Swords, Stanford and Company, 1935), 130–31.

different and in unforeseen places is at the heart of mission — as it is also at the heart of a Christian engagement with the MDGs. Moving beyond parochialism and provincialism in lives of worship, forgiveness, proclamation, service, and justice making, we are called to risk ourselves for the sake of God's reconciled creation. There is no more important work for each of us, individually and corporately, than to risk ourselves for the sake of God's mission. What can one person do? One person can participate in the mission of God. If not us, as the followers of Christ, then who? If not now, then when?

?? QUESTIONS FOR DISCUSSION

◆ In what ways do you participate in God's mission? What else might you do to further this mission?

◆ To what extent do you think it is possible to share a Christian mission with those of other faiths? Is conversion to Christianity a necessary objective of Christian mission?

MDGs

Goal 1: Eradicate extreme poverty and hunger

The aim of the first goal is, by 2015, to cut in half the proportion of people (starting at the 1990 proportion) whose income amounts to less than a dollar a day, and who suffer from hunger. About 1.1 billion people had less than $1 to spend today, and 852 million people were hungry. Let us be clear that poverty refers to deprivation — in health, education, nutrition, or income. This first goal focuses on "income poverty" and hunger.

Doesn't a dollar buy a lot in other countries?

One dollar, in this case, is measured not by how much we would get for $1 if we spent it in another country, but by how much $1 would buy in our hometown. This is known as "purchasing power parity" (PPP). For example, $1 might buy a loaf of bread in the US, although in Peru it might buy 10 loaves. However, to enable comparisons across countries, a person living on PPP$1 a day in Peru could buy only one loaf. To be precise, the "one dollar a day" comparisons are always based on what $1.08 would have bought in the United States in 1993.

Poverty data are still very rough and imperfect. This is true especially for income measures, but it also applies to measures of hunger, education, maternal mortality, etc. The statistics that we use are compiled by the World Bank, the Food and Agricultural Organization, the World Health Organization, and others. They draw upon the best internationally comparable estimates, and are updated regularly.

Income poverty: Halve those living on less than $1 a day.

Monetary income is not a perfect measure of poverty. In some areas people can supplement their income by growing their own food, or enjoy public goods such as water or electricity. Yet in many more areas those who live on less than $1 a day cannot supplement this income. They may be landless laborers or live in urban slums or not have access to public goods. Income may not be not a perfect measure of poverty, but when supplemented by the other MDGs, it is very useful.

Escape from poverty is not a matter of working harder, since the majority of the "extreme poor" work. Indeed they can be some of the busiest, hardest-working people in the world. The barriers they face often include not having an education, decent work, access to credit, or basic health care.

Where do the income poor live? Two-thirds of the world's poor people live in Asia, and most of the rest live in Africa. You might be surprised that, relatively speaking, Latin America is less impoverished than other areas.

In income poverty we see a pattern that recurs in many of the MDGs: **the number of poor persons is greatest in Asia, but the proportion of poor persons is greatest in Africa.** In India, 35 percent of the people live on less than $1 a day, but in Zambia, for example, it is 63 percent, and in Nigeria, 70 percent.

Undernourished 2000–2002

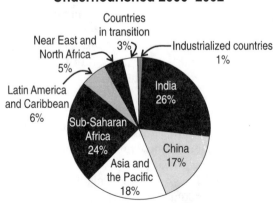

Source: Food and Agricultural Organization,
State of Food Insecurity 2004.

Hunger

The other part of Goal 1 is to halve the proportion of people who suffer from hunger. Hunger in this context is measured in relation to the prevalence of undernourishment and the prevalence of child malnutrition.

Over 850 million people are undernourished. Over 60 percent of these people live in Asia. In India alone 221 million are hungry — more than the entire continent of Africa. In many countries in Africa, however, the proportion of people who are undernourished is much higher. The worst is in Eritrea, where around 73 percent of the population are undernourished.

Hunger kills 5 million children a year, and 60 percent of all child deaths are related to malnutrition.

Hunger is a huge and painful issue that has not received its due attention, even among those who work on poverty. It is also solvable, and worth solving.

Ending hunger would even make good economic sense, for it would unleash $120 billion in economic growth in developing countries.[9] What is lacking, as the quote by Drèze and Sen in the introduction suggested, is public outcry — and public action.

QUESTION FOR DISCUSSION

◆ Few if any of us in this discussion consider ourselves to be "rich," but by the world's standards, we inevitably are. What do we take for granted that more than 1 billion (a sixth of the world's population!) consider as luxury?

9. Food and Agricultural Organization (FAO), *The State of Food Insecurity in the World* (Rome: FAO, 2004), 13.

ACTION 2:
STUDY, GET WISDOM, GET INSIGHT

The beginning of wisdom is this: Get wisdom,
and whatever else you get, get insight. (Proverbs 4:7)

How do we learn what God's mission is with respect to extreme poverty? One way is to study — both the grounds of our faith and our world that impoverishes so many. We can then try to cross this frontier wisely and with insight.

This action asks you to organize a study group on a Christian response to global poverty. A first step is to find a resource for critical thinking. To start you could choose this or another book or film on global poverty that members of the group can study and meet together to discuss.

Why is this strategic?

For effective Christian engagement on poverty, there is a need to speak to the mind as well as to the heart. There is a clear role for theological education regarding poverty, which is so often lacking in the church's response. And poverty is a problem of this world that, as such, demands creative, specific solutions.

A study group is an excellent way to learn together as a springboard for wise action. Although we are more aware of global poverty than previous generations there is still considerable ignorance and misinformation, both in terms of the extent of poverty and what can be done to reduce it. What is more, we may not know where our ignorance lies. For example, did you know before starting this book that 5 million children die each year of hunger?

The facts, figures, and ideas about poverty throughout this book need digesting. In order to turn this information into knowledge, and knowledge into wisdom, we need the opportunity to process the information and think it through. In a study group members can process the insights, respond to them, and share them with their family, friends, colleagues, and neighbors. Some might preach, teach, speak, or take a stand within their workplace on the subject, and perhaps influence scores of people. By reading and learning together, we are able to make an honest and persuasive case to others so that they too respond. Such a transmission of information can create a ripple effect, changing the outlook of an entire community.

A study group can bridge prayer, study, and practical action. Members can study the specifics of impoverishment and its causes, and learn

Jim Wallis:
Without Justice the Bible Is Full of Holes.
See for Yourself!

In his recent book God's Politics, *Wallis retells the story of how he discovered that poverty and justice were central themes in the Bible. It wasn't in church — it was during his first year in seminary.*

Here's what we did. Our band of eager young first-year seminary students...scoured the Old and New Testaments for every single reference to poor people, to wealth and poverty, to injustice and oppression, and to what the response to all those subjects was to be for the people of God.

We found *several thousand* verses in the Bible on the poor and God's response to injustice. We found it to be the second most prominent theme in the Hebrew Scriptures....One of every sixteen verses in the New Testament is about the poor or the subject of money....In the first three (Synoptic) gospels it is one out of ten verses, and in the book of Luke, it is one in seven!

After we completed our study, we all sat in a circle to discuss how the subject had been treated in the various churches in which we had grown up. Astoundingly, but also tellingly, not one of us could remember even one sermon on the poor from the pulpit of our home churches. In the Bible, the poor were everywhere; yet the subject was not to be found in our churches.

—Jim Wallis, *God's Politics: Why the Right Gets It Wrong and the Left Doesn't Get It* (San Francisco: HarperSanFrancisco, 2005), 212.

about and prepare concrete responses to it. It is a creative and extremely powerful community response.

How do you do it? Here are some suggestions about organizing a study group:

Find other readers and a place to meet

+ **At church:** Many churches have established book groups or adult education forums. If this is the case at your church, approach the organizer and suggest a series on global poverty.

♦ **At home:** You can also host a group at your home. Cast your net among your friends, coworkers, and parishioners in order to form your group. The level of interest is more important than size. Smaller groups allow more in-depth discussion while larger groups enable a wider diversity of reactions and opinions.

Establish a format for the discussion

♦ **Number of meetings:** Choose how many times to meet — perhaps over four to eight weeks, or during a specific season such as Advent, Epiphany, or Lent.

♦ **Discussion leaders:** Ask different group members to lead the discussion on different chapters. This reduces the burden on one person and can act as a model because members take turns being teachers and engaged learners. Leaders might give a brief overview of the chapter, then invite others to react. They might also prepare a few questions in advance to stimulate conversation and take the discussion deeper.

♦ **Mood:** When you ask a discussion question, be aware that people work out answers in different ways. Some need a moment of quiet to organize their thoughts, whereas others talk their way to an answer. Try to allow for both approaches. If simply waiting in silence for an answer seems too awkward, consider passing out paper and pencils and giving everyone a couple of minutes to jot down their thoughts on a particular issue.

The essential question, which should come at the end of the group's discussions, is "What now?" Reading about global poverty is just a point of departure. After learning about the issues, the group should allow time to plan possible responses. This is a perfect opportunity to decide how to engage with global poverty at both the personal and, if appropriate, the church level. The group may also explore how to press for greater involvement on the part of larger church structures and/or the national government. It is also an ideal time to learn what avenues already exist within the church or community for combating global poverty and determining if these are adequate or need to be expanded.

Books for discussion groups

The Bible. Try to repeat Jim Wallis's exercises (see p. 57) — even if it is just for one Gospel or one book of the Bible rather than the whole thing.

Chester, Tim, ed., *Justice, Mercy and Humility: Integral Mission and the Poor* (Carlisle, UK, and Waynesboro, Ga.: Paternoster Press, 2002). Produced by the Micah Network, this book outlines an evangelical framework for engagement and advocacy on the MDGs.

Curtis, Mark, *Trade for Life: Making Trade Work for Poor People* (London: Christian Aid, 2001). A study on one aspect of poverty reduction from Britain's largest Christian development agency.

Elliot, Charles, *Praying the Kingdom: Towards a Political Spirituality* (London: Darton, Longman and Todd, 1985). A book on intercessory prayer relating to social justice issues.

Griswold, Frank, *Going Home: An Invitation to Jubilee* (Cambridge, Mass.: Cowley Publications, 2001). A contribution by the presiding bishop of ECUSA.

Hoppe, Leslie J. *There Shall Be No Poor among You: Poverty in the Bible.* Nashville: Abingdon Press, 2004.

Hunter, Susan, *Black Death: AIDS in Africa* (New York: Palgrave Macmillan, 2003). This accessible book brings readers up to date on the HIV/AIDS crisis in Africa, describes what Africans are doing on the ground, and what others can do to help.

Marshall, Katherine, and Lucy Keough, *Mind, Heart, and Soul in the Fight against Poverty* (Washington, D.C.: World Bank, 2004). Each chapter of this book documents an example of how faith groups can and have worked in the area of development.

Myers, Bryant, *Walking with the Poor: Principles and Practices of Transformational Development* (Maryknoll, N.Y.: Orbis Books, 1999). As a vice president of World Vision, where he worked for twenty years, Myers writes for Christians who wish to do development work that is holistic, constructive, and sensitive, and gives witness to their faith.

Presler, Titus, *Horizons of Mission* (Cambridge, Mass.: Cowley Publications, 2001). Using stories as well as description, this book provides an overview of the history, theology, and practice of Christians participating in God's mission and was written specifically for church study groups.

Reed, Charles, ed., *Development Matters: Christian Perspectives on Globalization* (London: Church House, 2001). A well-informed response by the Church of England to globalization, with much on poverty.

Rough Guide to a Better World, A. Although not specifically Christian, this is an excellent and accessible resource for churches and would appeal to a younger audience. Produced by the Department for International Development in the UK, it is available free from post offices in the UK.

Sachs, Jeffrey, *The End of Poverty: How We Can Make It Happen in Our Lifetime* (London and New York: Penguin, 2005). A popular and passionate introduction to the thinking of the special advisor to the UN secretary-general on the MDGs.

Sider, Ronald J., *Rich Christians in an Age of Hunger* (Nashville: W Publishing Group, 2005). A classic book, frequently revised and reprinted, coming from an evangelical perspective.

Sider, Ronald J., Philip N. Olson, and Heidi Rolland Unruh, *Churches That Make a Difference: Reaching Your Community with Good News and Good Works* (Grand Rapids: Baker Books, 2002). This book provides case studies of churches that combine spiritual and social ministries and gives steps churches can take to transform themselves. Useful as a study guide for churches wishing to engage in local (mostly) and global mission.

Sustainable Human Development: A Young People's Introduction (London: Peace Child International, 2002). A study book for teenagers (or the young at heart!) based on the United Nations *Human Development Reports.*

Voices of the Poor. A three-volume compendium of insights from the poor from around the world. An excellent resource that can be downloaded on the Internet from *www.worldbank.org/empowerment.*

Williams, Jessica, *50 Facts That Should Change the World* (Thriplow, UK: Icon Books, 2004). A secular book by a journalist whose list of shocking facts contains many to do with poverty and development issues. It's not an in-depth study, but would provide a good source for stimulating discussion.

In addition, organizations such as Oxfam, World Vision, Catholic Fund for Overseas Development, and Christian Aid regularly produce useful study books and packs, and it is worth visiting their Web sites.

3

"When Did We See You?" — Justice and Judgment

Bono: A Revolt against Indifference

Celebrities from the arts have done much to draw the world's attention to global poverty. One of the most prominent is Bono, lead singer for the rock group U2.

What do rock stars like me have to contribute to debates about global poverty, the international debt burden on developing countries, and HIV/AIDS? I think we can help tell the story better. We can help, for example, in the area of branding, because rock stars have above all to build their own brands.

We need to get much better at branding in the area of poverty. We have to dramatize the story. We have to shape a clear melody line, or the public will fall asleep in the comfort of their freedom, as indeed I did for many years....

I am talking about a shift in global consciousness. It should feel like a revolt, because it is — against our own indifference. Branding would help dramatize the plight of the world's poor, help wake up people in the United States and Europe to the fact that poverty is not moral or acceptable.

Churches have a special role to play here. They have spheres of influence that reach widely and deeply. Frankly speaking, they also have great "stage gear." I recall well a photograph with His Holiness Pope John Paul II in Castelgandolfo, the Pope's summer residence, that helped us publicize the international Jubilee 2000 campaign to cancel the debt of developing countries. When campaign leaders went to Castelgandolfo, the Pope swiped my sunglasses. He put them on for a moment, which I will remember for the rest of my life as it showed great humor and grace. Then he read a remarkable tract about commitment to social justice.

The photograph of us together on this occasion, sadly not with my spectacles on, helped immeasurably in dramatizing the enormous challenges of poverty, debt, and HIV/AIDS. People began to say, "What are they doing hanging out together? This must be important...."

Clearly there is great momentum behind the Millennium Development Goals, but it is not enough to get us where we need to go. It seems like it would take an act of God to win this battle, to secure a shift in paradigm, a shift in the way we see the world, but perhaps it would not. It is we who have to act.

I might even say that God is on his knees, begging us to act, to get up off our behinds — and I include myself in this — and take this fight against world poverty to a new level.

— Quoted in Katherine Marshall and Richard Marsh, eds.,
Millennium Challenges for Development and Faith Institutions
(Washington, D.C.: World Bank, 2003), 12–13.

Recall for a moment the vivid picture of Christ that is portrayed in the parable of the separation of sheep and goats found toward the end of Matthew's Gospel (Matthew 25:31–46). The parable looks to the future, telling of Christ's second coming. In the story, Christ the Son of Man returns to us not as the wandering preacher, teacher, healer, and carpenter's son from the backwater town of Nazareth, but as a king enthroned in splendor attended by angelic courtiers. No longer is his audience the curious people of Galilee or the baying crowds of Jerusalem. Spread before the king is a vast crowd gathered from all the nations. Indeed, the crowd consists of every human being that has ever lived. The king addresses his audience, commending those who cared for the Son of Man when he was in need. Having no recollection of caring for such a person, or perhaps thinking he must have been disguised, the crowd is confused and asks:

> Lord, when was it that we saw you hungry and gave you food, or thirsty and gave you something to drink? And when was it that we saw you a stranger and welcomed you, or naked and gave you clothing? And when was it that we saw you sick or in prison and visited you?

To which the king replies with a telling remark, "Truly I tell you, just as you did it to one of the least of these who are members of my family, you did it to me."

This parable is rich in meaning and has inspired generations of Christians to care for the poor and marginalized. This chapter ponders this passage and probes its depths. It begins by tracing the story's concern for the poor. It then moves to the second, less comfortable, part of the parable and considers in what sense we are under judgment. It closes by turning again to the MDGs and drawing the ties between these goals and concrete actions that witness to love and hope. As we consider this parable from these different angles it is hard not to feel the force of

St. Francis of Assisi's command, "Preach the Gospel at all times. Use words if necessary."

This chapter draws repeatedly on biblical perspectives from the global South, for those who actively work to reduce poverty are not the only ones to engage with scripture. People living in poverty do so as well. It is crucial for us to listen to, and reflect upon, their insights as they seek to apply Jesus' teaching within their own context. We discount their perspectives at our peril.

The option for the poor

Return to the scene above—of the Son of Man, in splendor, addressing all humanity. The scene conveys vividly that those who are righteous in God's sight are those who care for the poor and marginalized, "the least of these who are members of my family." If this were not guidance enough, the parable expresses that in caring for the poor and marginalized we care for Christ himself. It is therefore a story about how we as people of faith can lovingly offer our lives to Christ. As the liberation theologian Gustavo Gutiérrez says of this passage, "It is not enough to say that love of God is inseparable from the love of neighbor. It must be added love for God is unavoidably expressed *through* love of one's neighbor. Moreover, God is loved in the neighbor."[1]

The close relationship between the Son of Man and those in need helps us make sense of what is often termed the "bias to the poor," touched upon in chapter 2. This bias occurs in many places in the Bible where those on the margins of society and those in greatest need are given an elevated position before God. This bias is not an argument in favor of poverty—far from it. Rather, it acknowledges God's proximity to, and special concern for, "the least of these." In terms used by the theologian C. E. B. Cranfield this is a story about the "Real Presence of the Risen Christ" in the poor and marginalized.[2] What Cranfield means is that it is a mystical presence in the same sense that Christ is present in scripture and the sacraments of the church. It is a statement about where God's presence can be authentically, yet mysteriously, witnessed and experienced. And just as we should treat the Word of God and the sacraments of the church with reverence, so should we treat with dignity and respect those who are impoverished or marginalized, for by doing so we honor God.

---

1. Gustavo Gutiérrez, *A Theology of Liberation* (Maryknoll, N.Y.: Orbis Books, 1973), 200.

2. Cited in Graham N. Stanton, *A Gospel for a New People: Studies in Matthew* (Edinburgh: T. & T. Clark, 1992), 209–10.

Theologians Agree:
The Option for the Poor Is Not Optional

"Medellín is the cradle of liberation theology. It is a clear and un-ambiguous assertion that the church should exert a 'preferential option for the poor' — an ideal that has become the hallmark of liberation theology."[a]

As Elsa Tamez, a theologian from Costa Rica, wrote, "The poor (men, women, blacks, Indians) . . . are in a privileged place, herme-neutically speaking," thus introducing an insight from liberation theology, namely, that scholars' interpretations of the biblical texts is partly colored by their economic, social, and political out-looks — and the insights of the poor have an important role in a balanced interpretation.[b]

"According to the Bible, it is central to the very nature of God to demand justice for the poor and oppressed. In light of this biblical teaching, how biblical is our theology? I think we must confess that rich Christians are largely on the side of the rich rather than the poor."[c]

a. Deane William Ferm, *Third-World Liberation Theologies: An Introductory Survey* (Eugene, Ore.: Wipf and Stock, 1986), 11.
b. Elsa Tamez, "Women's Rereading of the Bible," in *Voices from the Margin: Interpreting the Bible in the Third World*, ed. R. S. Sugirtharajah (London: SPCK, 1991).
c. Ronald Sider, *Rich Christians in an Age of Hunger*, 20th anniversary revision (Nashville: W Publishing Group, 1997), 65.

This raises the question, Why should the poor and marginalized be special in the sight of God? At times poverty heightens one's sense of ultimate dependence upon God. In his enthronement sermon the Angli-can archbishop of Canterbury, Rowan Williams, put it in these terms: "For those who know their need, God is immediate — not an idea, not a theory, but life, food, air for the stifled spirit and the beaten, despised, exploited body."[3]

3. *www.archbishopofcanterbury.org/sermons_speeches/2003/030227.html.*

"Jesus' mission is a holistic mission to the poor."[d]

"Christianity has sided with all that is weak and base, with all failures; it has made an idea of whatever *contradicts* the instinct of the strong life to preserve itself."[e]

Jim Wallis interprets the biblical saying "the poor you will always have with you" by writing, "Remember the context. They are at the dinner table with a leper, and Jesus is making an assumption about his disciples' continuing *proximity* to the poor. He is saying, in effect, 'Look, you will always have the poor with you' *because* you are my disciples. You know who we spend our time with, who we share meals with, who listens to our message, who we focus our attention on. You've been watching me, and you know what my priorities are. You know who comes first in the kingdom of God. So, you will always be near the poor, you'll always be with them, and you will always have the opportunity to share with them."[f]

"This gospel proclamation that convenes a church flows out of a decision to side with the interests and struggles of the poor and exploited classes in a real and active way."[g]

---

d. Bryant Myers, *Walking with the Poor: Principles and Practices of Transformational Development* (Maryknoll, N.Y.: Orbis Books, 1999).

e. Friedrich Nietzsche, one of Christianity's harshest critics, in "The Antichrist"; cited in Dorothee Soelle, *Suffering,* trans. Everett Kalin (Philadelphia: Fortress Press, 1975), 160.

f. Jim Wallis, *God's Politics: Why the Right Gets It Wrong and the Left Doesn't Get It* (San Francisco: HarperSanFrancisco, 2005), 210.

g. Gustavo Gutiérrez, "Liberation Praxis and Christian Faith," in *Frontiers of Theology in Latin America,* ed. Rosino Gibellini (Maryknoll, N.Y.: Orbis Books, 1979; London: SCM Press, 1980), 260.

Also, many biblical texts suggest that God is especially concerned for the poor on the grounds of justice. *Anawim* is one of the Hebrew words used to designate the poor and marginalized, and in the Hebrew scriptures (the Old Testament) the *anawim* are consistently portrayed as especially beloved of God because the God of justice cares for them and is distressed when they suffer. For example, Deuteronomy 24:14–15 gives very practical guidance as to how to treat the poor: "You shall not withhold the wages of poor and needy laborers, whether other Israelites or aliens who reside in your land in one of your towns. You shall pay them their wages daily before sunset, because they are poor and their livelihood depends on them; otherwise they might cry to the Lord against you, and you would incur guilt." As the Indian theologian George Soares-Prabhu has written, *anawim* stands "for those whom poverty and powerlessness have taught 'to bend before God' and place their trust in him alone."[4]

This understanding of God's concern for, and presence among, the poor is the inspiration behind liberation theology, as Leonardo and Clodovis Boff, two leading exponents, explain:

> Every true theology springs from a spirituality — that is, from a true meeting with God in history. Liberation theology was born when faith confronted the injustice done to the poor. By "poor" we do not mean the poor individual who knocks on the door asking for alms. We mean a collective poor. . . . In the light of faith, Christians see in them the challenging face of the Suffering Servant, Jesus Christ. At first there is silence, silent and sorrowful contemplation, as if in the presence of a mystery that calls for introspection and prayer. Then this presence speaks. The Crucified in these crucified persons weeps and cries out: "I was hungry . . . in prison . . . naked" (Matt. 25:31–46).[5]

At first sight, the thrust of the parable seems crystal clear: Christians are called to respond to those in need. Yet among theologians Matthew 25:31–46 is a controversial passage. Since at least the third century scholars have argued whether Jesus' qualifying phrase, "members of my family," speaks only of Christians — members of the family of the church — who are in need, or whether it embraces all humanity. But even those who favor the first interpretation find it hard not to see a universal message of care and compassion in this passage. New Testament scholar Graham Stanton argues that the Gospel writer had suffering Christians very much in mind when recounting this story. But Stanton also says, "On theological grounds I am predisposed to read Matthew 25:31–46 as a solemn exhortation to the church (and indeed to all men and women) to give priority to the hungry, thirsty, and needy of the world."[6]

Matthew 25:31–46 is not only a call to care for those in need and a reminder of what should be our priorities as disciples of Christ. First

---

4. George Soares-Prabhu, "Class in the Bible: The Biblical Poor a Social Class?" in *Voices from the Margin: Interpreting the Bible in the Third World*, ed. R. S. Sugirtharajah (London: SPCK, 1991), 150.

5. Leonardo Boff and Clodovis Boff, *Introducing Liberation Theology* (Maryknoll, N.Y.: Orbis Books; Tunbridge Wells, UK: Burns & Oates, 1987).

6. Stanton, *A Gospel for a New People*, 211.

and foremost the parable is a story about judgment, the climax to a long section of teaching in the Gospel that brings us face-to-face with God's ultimate purpose for humankind. Yet so often we water down this story by omitting its dramatic ending. The parable concludes with the king warning that he will separate the righteous and unrighteous as a shepherd would separate sheep from goats. Those who fail to respond to the least of these "will go away into eternal punishment, but the righteous into eternal life." These are the words of Jesus the prophet. This passage, and its dire warning, is a refrain of Hebrew prophecy, in which the establishment of a society on the twin pillars of justice and righteousness is a running theme — as is judgment. Jesus' words echo Isaiah's clarion call for expressing faith in social action, which in turn has been taken up by Christians from the days of the early church to the Jubilee 2000 movement of recent times:

> Is not this the fast that I choose:
> to loose the bonds of injustice,
> to undo the thongs of the yoke,
> to let the oppressed go free,
> and to break every yoke?
> Is it not to share your bread with the hungry,
> and bring the homeless poor into your house;
> when you see the naked, to cover them,
> and not to hide yourself from your own kin? (Isaiah 58:6–7)

Matthew 25 brought one leading activist, the American Jim Wallis, back to the Christian faith. Here is one of his observations about it:

> What's always been most striking to me is that the people gathered in front of the throne of Christ in this story all really believe they are among his followers. And they must be completely stunned to learn that they will be separated and judged by how they have treated the poor — the poor! This judgment is not about right doctrine or good theology, not about personal piety or sexual ethics, not about church leadership or about success in ministry. It's about how we treated the most vulnerable people in our society, whom Jesus calls "the least of these."[7]

---

7. Wallis, *God's Politics*, 217.

◆ How do you respond to Bible passages that give a bias to the poor?

Beyond fear and guilt

If we are to follow Jesus' and the prophets' call to work for justice and to proclaim a God of justice, then we must take seriously a fundamental aspect of justice, which is the need for judgment. Justice cannot be administered without judgment, since judgment determines what is and what is not just. In church circles (and among many people of goodwill), much is spoken of justice — and much is done in the name of justice — yet there is often a deafening silence on the subject of judgment.

In some respects this is a good thing. Throughout history, churches have from time to time used the fear of judgment as a tool for aggressive and insensitive evangelism — and for keeping its members in line. Medieval images of a fiery hell and places of torment gave a particularly frightening slant on the negative consequences of judgment and of what is meant by "eternal punishment." Furthermore, an overemphasis on judgment not only sits uncomfortably with our understanding of a loving and reconciling God, but it can be harmful both spiritually and psychologically. Many people reject Christianity because they perceive it to be judgmental, rather than accepting of human fallibility and supportive of personal development and transformation. Fear of judgment can induce forms of Christian discipleship that are negative and stifling, based on guilt and punishment-avoidance, rather than the light and hope of Christ and the liberating power of the Spirit.

For understandable but misguided reasons, judgment also sits uncomfortably with a secular, postmodern outlook on life, which plays down or denies the possibility of moral absolutes. The moral playing field is further complicated by the growth of multicultural and multifaith societies where our minds are opened to other perspectives. On issues such as sexual ethics, business ethics, or stewardship, where there is no ethical consensus, it becomes difficult to judge "good and bad" or "right or wrong." These factors would seem to make a heavenly judicial system appear grossly unfair. Yet rather than making us shy away from the image of God as judge, these should invite us to take the search for truth — and the understanding of our potential biases — more seriously.

We cannot escape the need for judgment if we are to proclaim a gospel of justice. Justice cannot be administered without judgment — of others and of ourselves.

As is so often the case, Christians understand what is meant by judgment in very different ways. This is not surprising, since the Bible is unclear about the exact nature of divine judgment, such as whether it will take place at a once-only event at the end of history, as some would have it, or whether it happens here and now in our daily lives, as others believe.

One healthy way to make sense of divine judgment is to look beyond the outdated medieval images of hell and physical punishment and to let go of an idea of judgment based on simplistic concepts of right and wrong, good and bad. Rather, by judgment we see and note the inconsistencies in how we live our God-given lives. Not only do we answer to God; our actions also affect the well-being of others, for whom God is equally concerned. Our actions also affect us — our character and fulfillment. We could view judgment not only as something that will take place in the future, but also as an ongoing process that guides us away from greed and indifference, toward joy and grace. We respond by offering ourselves to a loving God here and now, seeking to discern and to do God's will.

Daily prayerful reflection on "what we have done or failed to do" is a discipline that the statesman and scientist Benjamin Franklin cultivated in what he called a "liturgy" of daily prayer. In the morning Franklin would ask himself, "What Good shall I do today?" and in the evening he would ask, "What Good have I done today?" It is also at the heart of the *Examen* that thirty-three-year-old former soldier Ignatius of Loyola learned when he withdrew to a grotto for nine months and asked God how to pray. The box on page 70 elaborates Ignatius's method.

Freed by truth

One biblical story that helps us to understand the positive dimension to judgment is the parable of the unjust judge in Luke 18:1–8. The parable tells the story of a widow who is seeking justice against her opponent. We are not told what the issue is, but perhaps she is owed money. In the society of the time widows were in a vulnerable position, as they were unable to inherit from their husbands and so were often reliant on the support of the community. This poor widow is unable to get a hearing from the judge, and so she pesters him until finally he gives in and hears her case and grants her justice. At one level, the parable is about the importance of persistent prayer. But, like the parable of the

A Spiritual Exercise

Many Christians have found Ignatius's examination of conscience to be a very helpful spiritual exercise. Some use it daily. Some use it once in a while — when they are on retreat or having a quiet day — to approach God as judge in a constructive and healthy way.

Here are the basic steps:

1. Come into God's presence. Thank God and bless God for God's goodness and loving-kindness.

2. Ask God to come and enlighten you to see yourself as God sees you — clearly, fully, and in a loving perspective.

3. Think over your day, hour by hour or place by place or by relationships, activities, thoughts. What did you do? What did you say? What feelings arise as you remember these things — gladness or tension? This is the heart of the exercise and takes a few days to learn to do but is well worth learning, for God can guide you. Be aware of when you felt authentic.

4. Discuss your day with the Lord — the good times, the stressful times, the times that felt out of sync, the times you missed the mark. Observe when you had been away or turned away from God, and when you felt attuned — even if you were not thinking about God all of the time! If appropriate, ask forgiveness for misdeeds. Turn to tomorrow — ask God's companionship to be with you during the day, and seek to be attuned to it, that it might be a spring of living water, bubbling up within to eternal life.

5. End in the Lord's Prayer.

Try this exercise, even if only for a few minutes. Does it help you to approach God as Truth and as judge in a positive way?

separation of sheep and goats, it is also about divine judgment. Here the widow — and many women today like her — symbolizes God's faithful people who are not afraid of God, but rather seek out God with hope and expectancy in order to be judged.

The archbishop of Canterbury, Rowan Williams, has done a great deal in recent years to rehabilitate the idea of divine judgment and to make it comprehensible to our generation. In a media interview about the war in Iraq, Williams refused to be drawn into making a moral assessment of UK prime minister Tony Blair's role in the decision to go to war, but instead stated that Tony Blair, like all of us, would answer for his actions "at the judgment seat." This may at first appear as a veiled threat, but it is not. For Williams goes right to the heart of the matter when he describes judgment as *confronting the truth*. Before God there is nothing we can hide; all will be revealed. In a sermon delivered to a circuit of judges in Wales, Williams gives this vivid description of God as judge: "The vision of God is the cornerstone of justice: when we know ourselves to be before God we know ourselves to be the object of a costly and careful attention, searching out the whole of our truth, accepting it and engaging with it; we experience the way that grace opens our eyes to what we'd rather not face in ourselves, gently brings us back to confront our failures honestly, gathers up what's fragmented and forgotten. In the light of that divine attention, we know what we must offer to each other and what we need from each other — truth sustained by grace."[8]

So by accepting God as judge, by being willing to be exposed to God's truth, our own judgment can be improved. Our own moral judgments may never be completely accurate and will always be prone to distortion, but this attitude and acceptance of judgment helps us, bit by bit, to grow in wisdom and understanding.

?? QUESTION FOR DISCUSSION

◆ What is your response to the quotation above in which "grace opens our eyes to what we'd rather not face"?

8. Rowan Williams, *Open to Judgement: Sermons and Addresses* (London: Darton, Longman and Todd, 1994), 243–44.

Justice and the MDGs

In the parable of the unjust judge, the judge granted justice to the persistent widow. As Jesus asks in Luke 18:7, "And will not God grant justice to his chosen ones who cry to him day and night?" Two of the MDGs also relate directly to women — women who might hope that God would take up their case. Goals 2 and 3 described below are about education, and Goal 3 relates to gender equality — particularly getting every girl into school. Goal 5, described in chapter 7, addresses the tragedy that over five hundred thousand women every year die in childbirth or of birth-related complications. The section below describes Goals 2 and 3 and our halting progress toward achieving them.

MDGs

Goal 2: Achieve universal primary education

Specifically, the aim of MDG 2 is, by 2015, to ensure that children everywhere, boys and girls alike, will be able to complete primary school. Over 120 million school-aged children — one out of seven — are not in school. And one-quarter of the children who go to primary school in low-income countries drop out before completing five years.

A good primary education has a disproportionately positive effect on a person throughout the rest of his or her life. However, only 2 percent of the total overseas development assistance is directed to basic education. Christ the Teacher has been an inspiration for Christians down the centuries to support education, and the churches have consistently advocated for support for education and been involved in its delivery.

Why education?

Education can be important for various distinct reasons.

*   Education can have **intrinsic value**. Women and men who can read and write can enjoy poetry and literature and explore their intellectual curiosities.

Education may also be **instrumentally** important because of these connections:

*   Education is **fundamental for health,** because children learn about health, nutrition, and sanitation at school. Schools may also be places where governments provide school meals and immunization to children.

- Education may lead to **better employment** opportunities for women as well as men.

- Education can **empower** people and enable them — through knowledge, public expression, and democratic debate — to promote their good and that of others.

- Children learn **values** at school — for good or ill. Schools may reinforce prejudices or traditional gender roles and encourage passivity or rote learning rather than proactive problem solving. But teachers and curricula may also foster honesty, sharing, self-confidence, and mutual respect; may transmit skills of mediation and social engagement; and may use educational methods that support girls' performance.

How are we doing so far?

Three regions — East Asia and the Pacific, Europe and Central Asia, and Latin America and the Caribbean — are on track to achieve the goal. The others are falling short. South Asia contains the greatest number of these young children without schools; Sub-Saharan Africa has the highest proportion of children out of school.

Regional distribution of primary-age children not in school, percentage of total, 2000

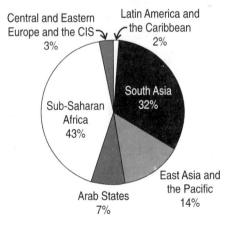

Central and Eastern Europe and the CIS
3%

Latin America and the Caribbean
2%

South Asia
32%

Sub-Saharan Africa
43%

Arab States
7%

East Asia and the Pacific
14%

Source: UNESCO, 2002.

Goal 3: Promote gender equality and empower women

Specifically, the target is to eliminate gender disparity in primary and secondary education, preferably by 2005 and to all levels of education no later than 2015.

Youth illiteracy 2000–2004
(percentage of 15–24-year-olds)

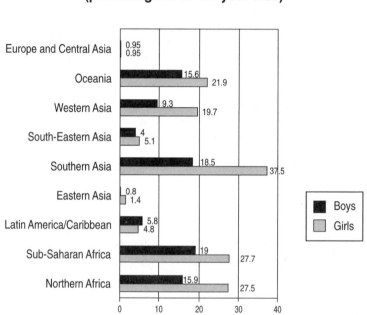

Source: United Nations Statistics Division, "World and Regional Trends," Millennium Indicators Database, *http://millenniumindicators.un.org*; based on data provided by UNESCO.

How are we doing so far?

Gender equality in primary education enrollment has been achieved in parts of the developing world. However, Southern Asia, Sub-Saharan Africa, and Western Asia lag considerably behind.

As is evident, young women in South Asia are by far the most illiterate in the world, followed by Sub-Saharan Africa and Northern Africa. Recent estimates show more girls in school, but most regions fall short of the target of eliminating gender inequality in primary and secondary education by 2005.

?? **QUESTION FOR DISCUSSION**

◆ Read Mary's Magnificat, found in Luke 1:46–55, and Hannah's prayer in 1 Samuel 2:1–10. How do you respond to these prayers for justice, delivered by women, in the light of the unequal burden women bear today in the world?

So what does the biblical account of divine justice have to do with our response to poverty? How does it shape the way we see ourselves, and how can it shape our conversations, our lessons, and the actions of our community? How should it affect our work for the Millennium Development Goals? Speaking at a rally on the MDGs in Trafalgar Square, London, in 2005, Nelson Mandela, one person who has done much to transform attitudes and lead humanity in the ways of freedom and justice, left his listeners with this inspiring account and call to action:

> Massive poverty and obscene inequality are such terrible scourges of our times — times in which the world boasts of breathtaking advances in science, technology, industry and wealth accumulation — that they have to rank alongside slavery and apartheid as social evils. The Global Campaign for Action Against Poverty can take its place as a public movement alongside the movement to abolish slavery and the international solidarity against apartheid.... Like slavery and apartheid, poverty is not natural. It is man-made and it can be overcome and eradicated by the actions of human beings. And overcoming poverty is not a gesture of charity. It is an act of justice. It is the protection of a fundamental human right, the right to dignity and a decent life....
>
> Sometimes it falls upon a generation to be great. You can be that great generation. Let your greatness blossom.[9]

Mandela makes a clear distinction between charity and justice — as have many others. Each of us must make the same distinction. Charity as it is used here means voluntary handouts or short-term gifts to help in an emergency — and this form of charity is not sufficient. Justice is obligatory.

---

9. From the speech "Make History. Make Poverty History," given February 3, 2005, at Trafalgar Square, London. The full text is available at *www.surefish.co.uk/campaigns/mph/030205_mph_mandela_speech.htm.*

This chapter has focused on judgment in Christian thinking and related it to addressing global poverty, particularly gender-based poverty. This is not to suggest that the only source of motivation for Christians to work for poverty reduction is the prospect of being judged. Surely just as important as the Golden Rule, "Do to others as you would have them do to you" (Luke 6:31; cf. Matthew 7:12), is an ethic of empathy which is explicitly found in the teachings of other faiths including Islam, Buddhism, Judaism, Hinduism, Baha'i, Confucianism, Sikhism, Jainism, and Zoroastrianism, and one which resonates powerfully with people of no faith. Also of crucial importance is Jesus' command that "You shall love your neighbor as yourself," which echoes Leviticus 19:18 and is expanded in the parable of the good Samaritan.

Nevertheless, we have argued that it is important not to underplay judgment as a motive for social action. We have also argued that it is important to understand what judgment is and is not. Judgment is about being exposed to the truth; it is not about being put on trial. Being exposed to the truth can be one of the most liberating experiences we can have, because it opens our eyes to realities that may have escaped us and can inspire us to respond to these realities alongside a wide community of individuals and churches around the world. Being exposed to the truth can indeed be a catalyst to make our "greatness blossom."

ACTION 3:
GIVE 0.7 PERCENT

Licensed to give: The 007 rule

There is an Indian proverb, "One who hears a story is blessed. One who tells a story is twice blessed." This same principle could be applied to financial giving. The one who has is blessed; the one who gives of what she has is twice blessed.

This action asks you to encourage others to commit at least 0.7 percent of their income to reduce poverty overseas — having already done so yourself. This action is directly strategic because people's private funds can be channeled directly to poverty-reducing activities (not all ODA addresses poverty). It is also strategic because if Christians and churches themselves are giving 0.7 percent overseas, we have the integrity to demand that our governments do likewise.

Financial giving is not the solution to global poverty — structural changes are vital and provide more durable transformations. Neither is financial giving the only way we can and perhaps should give (see

How do I calculate
0.7 percent of my income?

Multiply
Income x .007 =
0.7 percent of my income

Income	0.7%	Income	0.7%	Income	0.7%
5	0.03	40,000	280	120,000	840
10	0.07	45,000	315	140,000	980
50	0.35	50,000	350	160,000	1,120
100	0.70	55,000	385	180,000	1,260
1,000	7	60,000	420	200,000	1,400
5,000	35	65,000	455	250,000	1,750
7,000	49	70,000	490	300,000	2,100
10,000	70	75,000	525	350,000	2,450
15,000	105	80,000	560	400,000	2,800
20,000	140	85,000	595	450,000	3,150
25,000	175	90,000	630	500,000	3,500
30,000	210	95,000	665	750,000	5,250
35,000	245	100,000	700	1,000,000	7,000

Action 4), but it is a constructive and essential component of an adequate response to poverty.

Encouraging others to give 0.7 percent

Money is a sensitive subject. As a Christian retreat program, Ministry of Money, observes, "Money is a paradox in our culture — it enslaves, yet it also frees; it is intensely private, but it is also very public; it measures worth, yet it is no measure of real worth; it destroys yet also creates."[10] One way to approach stewardship sensitively is to start by sharing accurate information about poverty and inequality, then by illustrating the impact that "giving 0.7 percent" can have.

These two steps can be an effective form of evangelism. The witness of Christians who understand God's concern for the poor and respond wisely and generously can communicate the Christian gospel very effectively simply by their lifestyle — the "sixty-seventh book of the Bible," as Myers says (see above p. 30). Also, evangelism literally means "bringing good news." The good news you bring is this: one person is trying to do what he or she can about global poverty — something that conveys compassion and brings change.

---

10. *www.ministryofmoney.org.*

Step 1. Accurate Information

The first step is to "share accurate information." It may be more precise to call it "correcting misinformation," for there are common assumptions that we are already doing all we can, that to redress poverty requires sacrificial levels of giving, or that money will do nothing to address the issue. Let's explore the first hunch — that we are doing all we can, that we are being very generous.

In the US, surveys have repeatedly shown that the widespread majority of citizens believe that the government spends *too much* on foreign aid and that an appropriate percentage of the budget would be 10 percent. **In fact the US gives the smallest proportion of any rich country and only 10 percent of what the American people think it does.** The US devotes less than 1 percent of its budget and only 0.16 percent of its GNI to bilateral foreign aid and development assistance, which amounts to 16 cents per day for each American. The US is the largest donor in terms of dollars spent (it is the largest economy, accounting for roughly one-third of the global economy), but it is almost the least generous in terms of the proportion of its national income (see the table on p. 36). Consistently, year after year, the US government gives far less than the American people think it does, proportionately less than most other nations give — and less also than we want it to.

Americans are a generous people. American foundations, corporations, and people give away over $240 billion a year. But how much of this goes overseas? **Less than 2 percent of American private philanthropy goes overseas.** This amounts to only $5.7 billion a year, or 5 cents a day for each American — and not all of this goes toward reducing poverty.

In the UK spending on overseas aid amounts to 23 cents (US) per person per day or 0.34 percent of GNI. It is estimated that 8.5 percent of the British public give overseas ordinarily, and that the *average* private **UK giving overseas is only 2 cents (US) per person per day** — or less than half of American private giving.

Step 2: Illustrate Impact

Your next task is to provide a few vivid examples of the impact of giving. Someone can, for example, choose to forego one large espresso drink per month and provide one child with the funds necessary to attend school for one year. Or someone can choose to substitute tap water for one can of soda daily and help fund the digging of a well so a village can have access to clean water. We have more power than we realize, but too often we allow our resources to be dissipated because we are busy and distracted and fail to examine our choices.

There are many examples; these are taken from World Vision, the world's largest Christian organization doing overseas development work:

- $25 ($2.09/month) can immunize a child against six lethal diseases and help provide health monitoring of the child and health training for mothers;

- $25 ($2.09/month) can provide a family with three insecticide-treated bed nets and information about preventing malaria (the WHO estimates that five hundred thousand African children could be saved every year through the use of these nets);

- $32 ($2.67/month) can supply one farming family with twelve pounds of drought-resistant seeds for crops like millet, sweet potatoes, and maize;

- $50 ($4.17/month) can send a child to school for a year;

- $100 ($8.34/month) will fund a micro-loan for an impoverished woman to start or expand a business that can provide for her family.

People often greet such figures with three responses. The first is doubt: **how could it cost so little?** Here we have to recognize that one dollar/ pound, if converted to rupees and spent in India (for example), will buy *far* more than one dollar/pound will buy here. That is why, when we compare income of people in different countries, economists always convert the income from "nominal" rates — which is what one dollar buys in another country — to "purchasing power parity" rates — which is the amount it costs to buy in India what one dollar/pound would buy in the US/UK (for example, a quart of milk; see p. 53). But because **the actual world runs in nominal terms**, your money goes a long way in many countries. For example, if you travel, you may stay in a luxury hotel for $30 a night, or buy a lovely meal for $2. This also means that the funds you send overseas go much further than you might expect, as the following story shows:

Shakeena Pathan had nowhere to turn after her husband deserted her and her to children. "I had no one to show me sympathy and love," the resident of Nagpur, a town in central India, said.

One of her friends, seeing her desperate plight, directed her to the Community Development Society loan program funded by Five Talents International. After attending entrepreneurship training, she chose to sell vegetables. Her loan was just $30, and with it she purchased a weighing scale and other necessary materials. After a few months of selling under a tree near the roadside, she is now able to net about $1 (nominal) each day. This means her two children have food on the table and shelter above their heads.[11]

A second response is mistrust: **how do I know my money isn't being wasted?** This is a huge issue, because there have been many scandals in which people's hard-earned, generously given money has been squandered. In response to such truly destructive mishaps in the past, some reputable organizations are now scrutinized by watchdogs, like *charitynavigator.org* — but you can also check them out yourself using this list of qualities that good organizations usually have:

+ Their mission/vision statement includes poverty reduction.

+ Their finances are in the black, not in the red.

+ A moderate percentage of their budget is spent on overhead and fundraising.

+ Their philosophy and methods are empowering rather than top-down and paternalistic.

+ They advocate and address the root causes of poverty.

+ Many of their staff are from the country in which they work.

+ Others who have observed their activities speak well of them.

A third response is: **how do I avoid being overwhelmed?** The other problem people often mention is their resentment of the floods of heartwrenching letters they receive asking for help. No sooner have they written a check to one group than they receive a dozen letters from others. Junk mail, unfortunately, is a huge issue because it induces guilt and sours people's goodwill (especially if "gifts" of stickers or cards are enclosed — which it is *not* unethical, in our view, to keep and to use).

Very practically, both in the US and the UK, you can write to the Direct Marketing Association (DMA)[12] and request that your address and/or

---

11. Reported by Craig Cole, Five Talents International, *www.fivetalents.org*.
12. US: Write to: MPS, Direct Marketing Association, P.O. Box 9008, Farmingville, NY 11735. UK: visit *www.mpsonline.org.uk*, or fax 020 7323 4226/tel 020 7291 3310, or write to Direct Marketing Association, DMA House, 70 Margaret Street, London W1W 8SS.

Pause for Self-Assessment

Try to estimate how much (as a percentage of your income), this year, you or your family has contributed financially overseas. Turn to the 0.7 percent chart (p. 77). Was it 0.7 percent? More? Less?

---

telephone number be removed from all mass mailing lists (saving both stress and paper). Spiritually, if you know that you make your stewardship decisions carefully and generously, then you need not be nagged by guilt. You may also talk through these things in a group without sharing private financial details. In one church, members found it was quite a liberating experience when one church leader broke the ice and shared, quite openly, the percentage of income the family gave, and how they made their decisions about how to divide it between the church and domestic and international organizations that serve the poor. In any case, if you give, then your own insights will become a resource to others, which is good because people may well ask you quite directly where you give, as they decide how and whether to do likewise.

Of course, if your chosen audience is children, you raise the topic of giving differently. For example, children can make "banks" or "mite boxes" where they save or divide their money between three compartments: one to spend, one to save, one to give away. Or you can make a donation in the name of a child, and give the child a "present" (e.g., a postcard notifying them that they have given a poor child's mother a goat — or whatever your donation supports). This establishes the habit and joy of generosity early on.

The fundamental insight of stewardship is that our resources or talents are not "ours" to do with what we like — even if we do nothing more for the poor. Our budgets should reflect our priorities, and by looking at your budget alone or with a partner you can double-check if it does indeed represent your priorities. In his book *Neither Poverty nor Riches* Craig Blomberg carefully studies the Hebrew Bible and New Testament texts that pertain to wealth and poverty. When he turns, briefly, to consider the implications of this study in light of global poverty statistics and giving patterns, he writes: "I hope that all readers, and particularly those who share my Christian commitment, may realize the substantial disparity between the biblical mandates and contemporary Christian

Q: How Do We Decide Where to Give?

This question comes up again and again. The answer? It depends on what kind of a giver you are at this time. People are different, and they go through different stages of giving through their lives. Our many different kinds of gifts build a balanced response. Below are four useful ways that individual people's gifts can support the MDGs.

- **Systemic Change.** I want to reduce the most poverty with my gift — even if that means providing unglamorous things like sanitation systems or health systems. I don't need any thank-you cards, newsletters, or new relationships — just less poverty in our world. **Examples: water pipes, teacher salaries, supervision systems for health workers.**

    Large-scale poverty reduction requires hidden investments — to set up educational systems, health-care systems, pensions — some run by better governments. Systemic change is not always sentimental or small scale. Yet without it we will never reach the MDGs. Sample Organizations: Oxfam, Global Fund for Children's Vaccines, United Nations agencies.

- **Issue-Focused.** I want to give my money and energy to advancing work on a certain issue. **Examples: AIDS, Trade, Hunger, Women, Children, US Giving.**

    Reducing poverty requires people who care and give money yet also are able to chat knowledgeably with friends,

practice. I hope, too, that all may be challenged to address the issues of stewardship of material possessions in their own lives, joyfully, . . . in recognition that a large part of our world today, not least within the church, may well be called to repent of past apathy and self-centered indulgence."[13]

---

13. Craig L. Blomberg, *Neither Poverty nor Riches: A Biblical Theology of Possessions,* New Studies in Biblical Theology 7 (Leicester: Apollos, 1999), 32.

to teach, or to lobby for action. Sample organizations that inform and advocate: Washington Office on Africa, Bread for the World, Christian Aid.

- **Relationship-Based.** I want to feel connected. I want to be able to picture the community to which I give, to write to them, pray with them, or maybe someday visit them or send a friend. **Examples: "Small is beautiful" grassroots projects, NGOs, parish partnerships, mission groups.**

    Reducing impoverishment is enriched by people who engage with their hearts. Also how better to renew our church than in people-to-people and parish-to-parish relationships that enlarge our capacity to love? Sample organizations: most church denominational giving is of this type; see also Global Giving and Netaid (reputable Web sites where you can choose a tiny project that needs support).

- **Volunteer or Professional Work Abroad.** I'd like to learn how to volunteer, or to work, or spend part of my vacations overseas. OR...I have skills I think could be useful directly — in the health professions or in engineering or in teaching or in church work or in information technology or journalism or something else.

    — Modified from the EGR booklet *Preach the Gospel at All Times.*

    See Action 4 (p. 100), where this is discussed at length and sample organizations are given.

Web sites of sample organizations

The process of deciding where to give can be fruitful, because the experience of learning about all of the good work that different organizations are already doing can be interesting. So it is worth spending an afternoon a year reading about different places to give so you discern where to give and understand and have confidence in the work of your chosen organization. Here are some Web sites of reputable, and very different, organizations that you might start with:

Bread for the World (*www.bread.org*) is a US Christian citizens' movement that lobbies in Washington, D.C., on hunger and related issues.

Christian Aid (*www.christianaid.org*) is a UK Christian citizens' organization that raises awareness and undertakes advocacy in the UK and also supports disaster relief and development activities abroad.

Tearfund (*www.tearfund.org*) is a UK evangelical development and aid agency.

Church denominations usually have at least one overseas mission or development organization as part of their ministry and rely upon donations by churches and members to continue these important ministries. Often these groups will also have activities or placements for those wishing to volunteer or work abroad. See online *www.doorsofhope.com/christian-connections/denominations.htm*.

Catholic Agency for Overseas Development (CAFOD): *www.cafod.org.uk*

Catholic Relief Services: *www.catholicrelief.org*

Episcopal Relief and Development: *www.er-d.org*

Lutheran World Relief: *www.lwr.org*

Methodist Relief and Development Fund UK: *www.mrdf.org.uk*

Mennonite Central Committee: *www.mcc.org/*

Presbyterian World Mission US: *www.pcusa.org/navigation/mission.htm*

Quaker:
  US: *www.afsc.org/*
  UK: *www.quaker.org.uk/peace/index.html*

Southern Baptist International Mission Board US: *www.imb.org/core/default.asp*

United Methodist Committee on Relief US: *http://gbgm-umc.org/umcor/*

GlobalGiving (*www.globalgiving.org*) is a Web site you can use to find and fund small projects. Whether it's education for Afghan women or clean water for Nigerian villages, the Web site introduces a range of funding options to donors who want to make an impact at the grassroots level.

Global Fund for Children's Vaccines (*www.unicefusa.org/gavi/*). You can give directly to confront an "old" problem that we still need to address energetically. It costs $17 to vaccinate a child for life.

Heifer International (*www.heifer.org*). Based on the idea of "passing on the gift," Heifer provides animals to poor families, who in turn donate the female offspring of animals they have received, so the gift continues. The organization serves millions of families in 115 countries.

Netaid (*www.netaid.org*). Focusing on wealthy countries, Netaid raises awareness about extreme poverty and promotes activities that empower and make a meaningful difference in the lives of the world's poorest people.

Oxfam (*www.oxfam.org*). Oxfam's work is dedicated to finding lasting solutions to poverty and suffering. Working in both advocacy and grassroots development, Oxfam works to advance a number of issues including trade, education, debt, health, HIV/AIDS, and gender inequality.

World Evangelical Alliance (*http://globalmission.org/*). Runs a very extensive site with short-term and long-term mission opportunities.

World Service Enquiry (*www.wse.org.uk*). Based in the UK, WSE posts three hundred job vacancies a month for skilled and experienced people to work overseas and also has resources for those wishing to go abroad.

Want to check out a different organization? There are many small organizations that are excellent. Use the criteria above to check them out! Also, **Charity Navigator** (*www.charitynavigator.org*) provides Web profiles of over twenty-nine hundred organizations. Charity Navigator works to guide intelligent giving. Charity Navigator does not accept any contributions from any charities they evaluate. In the UK see the **UK Charity Commission** (*www.charity-commission.gov.uk*).

4

Who Are the Poor?

The First Telephone Lady

An important principle for meeting the MDGs is that those living in poverty should be empowered to lift themselves out of poverty. The Grameen Bank in Bangladesh, founded by Muhammad Yunus, has pioneered the provision of micro-credit among the poor for this purpose.

On Wednesday, March 26, 1997, Laily Begum did what millions of people around the world did on that day and do each and every day. She did something that most of us reading this take for granted: she made a call on a cell phone.

So what was so special about that call that I should write about it? Well, first of all Laily was phoning the prime minister of her country — Bangladesh. It's not every day that a woman like Laily picks up the phone and speaks to the head of her government! But that's not the reason that I'm telling you about it now.

There are two far more important things to say about Laily and what she did that day.

First of all, you should know that Laily is poor. She lives in the village of Patira, north of Dhaka, in Bangladesh, one of the poorest countries in the world. In Bangladesh, phones are rare, and only the well-off can afford them. In 1997, when Laily made that call, there were only 400,000 phones in Bangladesh — a country with a population of 120 million. That's one phone for every three hundred people. And most of those phones are in towns and cities, where the wealthier people live. So millions of poorer people like Laily living in rural areas have never seen a phone, let alone used one.[1] So not surprisingly, Laily's phone call was special because it was her first — and how many people can say that their first phone call was to a prime minister?

But it was special most of all for another reason, for on that day Laily became Bangladesh's first "telephone lady" — something that could make her

---

1. It is estimated that more than 70 percent of the world's population have never heard a dial tone. Jessica Williams, *50 Facts That Should Change the World* (Thriplow, UK: Icon Books, 2004), 190.

as famous as the person she called! It has certainly made Laily famous in her village — and not only famous, but important.

Communications in rural Bangladesh are very poor. This means it's difficult for people to keep in touch with their families and friends or to get messages to anyone who lives any distance away. Sending a message can take a lot of time and effort, because it means sending a messenger — who might have to take time away from work or studies to deliver the message. And if the message is urgent — perhaps a request for medical help — it may be too late by the time the message arrives. That's not the only problem. Many people in rural Bangladesh live isolated lives, especially women. They can find it difficult to make friends with other women in other villages — or to get help if they are abused.

So Laily is an important person in her community, because she has a cell phone. Using Laily's phone is the village's quickest, easiest, and most efficient way to keep in touch with the wider world. Laily's phone can help the people of Patira in so many ways.

The reason Laily has a cell phone is because she's a borrower from the Grameen Bank, which I set up to help the poorest of the poor in my country lift themselves out of poverty by their own enterprise. The bank offers micro-credit — small loans — to 4.5 million poor people in Bangladesh to help them get out of poverty, and 96 percent of the borrowers are women. The bank helps people like Laily, who are poor for no other reason than a lack of opportunity to get work which will pay a decent wage. Laily now has an opportunity, because as part of a new venture — GrameenPhone — she can make a living by letting other people in her village use the phone for a small charge.

But, of course, Laily and her phone wouldn't be of much use to the people in her village if there are only a few people in the country with phones. And so GrameenPhone is helping thousands of others to have phones so that they can set up a new national communications network across the country that connects families and friends, saves time and energy — and lives — and lifts people out of isolation. Today GrameenPhone has over 3 million subscribers, and Grameen Bank has over 100,000 telephone ladies all over Bangladesh.

Using cell phones in this way is an example of how relatively inexpensive technology can solve problems the poor have faced for centuries and transform people's lives. Technology also helps to overcome what could have been a major difficulty for the enterprise, which is that many villages in Bangladesh are without electricity. Fortunately, one thing Bangladesh is blessed with in abundance is sunlight! So where there is no electricity to charge the phone's battery, the phone can be powered by solar energy instead. We created a solar energy company called Grameen Shakti (or Energy) to sell solar panels to people who wish to have electricity in their homes or businesses.

Using cell phones in this way is such a simple idea that can make such a difference to so many people. For this reason I am very grateful to Iqbal, a young Bangladeshi American who came to see me in 1994 with the idea of using cell phones in Bangladesh.

So maybe the next time you get annoyed with someone for disturbing you by using a cell phone, you'll spare a thought for Laily, and for her fellow telephone ladies — and for all those people in Bangladesh whose lives have been transformed because they — like so many of us — can make a phone call.

— Muhammad Yunus, founder of the Grameen Bank

"The person who sleeps by the fire knows best how intensely it burns, so runs an Asante proverb."[2] In order to write this book we needed to find a term by which to refer to the people who *are* undernourished; the children who *are not* in primary school; the children and mothers who *do* perish needlessly; women who *are* excluded; those who *are* victims of HIV/AIDS, TB, and malaria; those who *do* dwell in slums or live without clean water and sanitation. We needed a term by which to speak about the persons to whom the first seven MDGs are directed — those who sleep by the fires of deprivation. We have chosen to call them "poor" or "impoverished." The term "impoverished" draws attention to the processes that perpetuate poverty; the term "poor" is also used simply because it is shorter and is the term others use. We recognize material poverty to be multidimensional and to include deprivations in health, education, income, nutrition, water, and so on. We refer to action in solidarity with the impoverished as "poverty reduction."

But who are "the impoverished"? So far we have usually spoken of "the poor" as people characterized by illiteracy, a lack of income, or an inability to protect themselves and their families from the ravages of even basic diseases. We have described "human poverty" with statistics and graphic stories, and these have focused our minds on material deprivations that we can and should work to redress. We have rehearsed different obligations upon Christians to respond. And yet such descriptions can seem cold, dehumanizing, and fundamentally *inaccurate*. They leave too much out.

If groups begin to talk about poverty, someone will eventually mention a problem. It is a problem exemplified in the vibrant energy of the telephone lady, and also in the following true story. A thoughtful, well-dressed American reflected that his grandmother had come from another

---

2. Mercy Amba Oduyoye, "Reflections from a Third-World Woman's Perspective: Women's Experience and Liberation Theologies," in *Feminist Theology from the Third World: A Reader*, ed. Ursula King (Maryknoll, N.Y.: Orbis Books, and London: SPCK, 1994), 24.

country. She was, it turned out, illiterate; his parents grew up without indoor plumbing and with smoky fires. His grandmother had lost three of her children before they reached their fifth birthday and had been widowed when her husband was killed by thieves. Yet the few times this man visited his grandmother as a child, he did not see her as poor. Sure, his parents would pack some extra food and try to think of excuses by which to give her warm clothes without offending her dignity. But she was, fundamentally, wise, capable, joyful, and beloved of her grandchildren because of her rich stories and deep laugh. She always insisted she had everything she needed, although every visitor could see she did not. During our discussion this man had been thinking that his grandmother might, by our description, be classified as among the "extreme poor" (which would have been literally true in that particular case), but she would not have been interested in that description. In fact, to describe her as "poor" would be to miss what was most important about her.

The liberation theologian Gustavo Gutiérrez instead describes the impoverished in this way: "The poor person is someone brimming over with capacities and possibilities.... We are talking about poor people who, despite the way they have been affected by circumstances (often seriously), resist all attempts to mutilate or manipulate their hopes for the future."[3]

This insight is crucial, which is why this chapter talks about how we, the relatively affluent, see the impoverished. It argues that too often through history the view of the impoverished held by those who have the resources to "help" has been flimsy and patronizing. This is as true in churches as elsewhere. For example, the history of the Christian missionary movement is riddled with examples of good and well-meaning people imposing their views, culture, and priorities on those with whom they shared the gospel. Too often the poor were viewed as objects of charity, not equals before God, and the goal of missionaries was to solve others' problems, not to empower others to act on their own behalf.

A more appropriate way to relate to the impoverished is to hold together several realities that are simultaneously true. One is that we stand in a position of relative economic affluence and power. God calls on all, especially on those of means, to respond generously to acute human suffering. Another is that the "poor" are exactly like us before God, people with strengths and with flaws, who will, like us, seek diverse kinds of

---

3. In Christopher Rowland, ed., *The Cambridge Companion to Liberation Theology* (Cambridge: Cambridge University Press, 1999), 25.

flourishing and live out their lives in many beautiful and reckless ways. In "reducing" poverty we must support people's God-given freedom to exercise their own vocations to serve, give, create, and lead. A third is that we are rich and poor in different dimensions at the same time. A person who is acutely poor in material terms may have wisdom, spiritual insight, or harmonious relationships that fulfill. Similarly, a person who is relatively "rich" in material terms may be foolish or bitter or lonely or insecure or insensitive. Neither the rich nor the poor are morally impeccable. Of course there are materially poor people who are foolish and rich people who are wise — but the point is that all of us are gifted in some ways and impoverished in others.

To build on the framework of chapter 2 we might ask, How do we participate in the mission of God with respect to persons who are materially deprived? We cannot fully answer this question, for God's work is deeply mysterious. God is beyond our comprehension and control, and we may be closest to God when we realize that we do not understand God's ways. Yet chapter 3 argued that poverty reduction does seem to be part of the justice God requires. So this section sets out one way in which poverty reduction could fit in as a vital and centrally important part — but only a part — of the saving purposes and actions of God with respect to the impoverished themselves. In the course of doing so it will also answer some concerns that Christians have: that "poverty reduction" is too focused on this world rather than on the eternal; that it concerns only the material aspects of life when Christians are called also to relational, ethical, and spiritual aspects of salvation; and that in some sense many of us are called to be poor or to find God through our suffering rather than to avoid suffering.

Human flourishing: Being free to love

Archbishop Oscar Romero reflected often that those who are "following Jesus" by working to redress social and economic deprivations need most to realize that their goal is not human justice, based on our limited sense of right or wrong, but something far more mysterious — the artwork of God:

> The liberation that Christianity preaches is a liberation from something that enslaves, for something that ennobles us.... The church ...struggles against the earth's enslavements, against oppression, against misery, against hunger. All that's true — but for what? For something. St. Paul uses a beautiful expression: to be free for love.

To be free for something positive, that is what Christ means when he says, "Follow me."[4]

One question we might ponder is how and when addressing extreme poverty makes the people involved more "free for love." If we try to see the bigger picture, then we can join our efforts with God's more accurately.

The starting point of Roman Catholic social teaching on poverty, which is one of the most systematic theological teachings on poverty, is the insight from Genesis that human beings are created in the image of God (*imago Dei*). Dignity is found in every child of God, "in all the unrepeatable reality of what he [or she] is and what he does, of his intellect and will, of his conscience and heart . . . of his personal being and also of his community and social being."[5] Extreme poverty is evil, intolerable, even appalling, because it denies people the outward goods which accord with their dignity as persons made in God's image.

Linking poverty reduction to cultivating the image of God (and understanding the image of God in a way that is accessible for women and men and children) fundamentally aligns it to a more holistic description of human nature and purposes than economic institutions generally advance. For example, the Micah Network, a group of mainly evangelical church alliances and development agencies, has, through a consultative process, developed and refined an understanding of "integral" mission — mission that serves people's material, spiritual, social, and intellectual aspects:

> It is not simply that evangelism and social involvement are to be done alongside each other. Rather, in integral mission our proclamation has social consequences as we call people of love and repentance in all areas of life and our social involvement has evangelistic consequences as we bear witness to the transforming grace of Jesus Christ. If we ignore the world we betray the word of God which sends us out to serve the world. If we ignore the word of God we have nothing to bring to the world. Justice and justification by faith, worship and political action, the spiritual and the material, personal change and structural change belong together. As in the

---

4. Excerpt from a sermon given October 14, 1979, in *The Violence of Love*, ed. James R. Brockman (Farmington, Pa.: Plough Publishing House, 1998), 170.

5. Pope John Paul II, encyclical letter *Redemptor Hominis* (London: Catholic Truth Society, 1979), section 14.

life of Jesus, being, doing, and saying are at the heart of our integral task.[6]

Recognizing the wider purposes of God for impoverished persons themselves also adds richness to our understanding of poverty reduction. Each person has a duty to use his or her talents to the glory of God. Reducing extreme poverty dignifies the impoverished and enables them to bring their own aptitudes and talents to fruition in the service of others.

Architects of change

Part of the image of God — and part of the fulfillment of persons — seems to be the enjoyment of various kinds of freedom, including the freedom to shape the lives we wish to lead, to be agents of our destiny, to act on our own behalf, and to direct our lives. Such is the value of these real freedoms that, many argue, it is appropriate to invest a great deal of time and energy in cultivating them. As the Micah Declaration puts it, "The poor like everyone else bear the image of the Creator. They have knowledge, abilities and resources. Treating the poor with respect means enabling the poor to be the architects of change in their communities rather than imposing solutions upon them."[7]

The importance of "enabling the poor to be the architects of change in their communities" cannot be overemphasized. Poverty reduction that prevents impoverished persons from developing and exercising their own vocations does indeed fall short of, if not stymie, the goal of human fulfillment. The mission movement was often discredited, and unfortunately left a sour taste for years to come, precisely because it did not enable the communities and persons concerned to develop their own systems for helping themselves.

Bryant Myers of World Vision insists that how we see and speak of the poor makes all the difference. He also observes: "The world tends to view the poor as a group that is helpless; thus we give ourselves permission to play god in the lives of the poor."[8] What would it look like to act differently? Consider the example in the box on page 93, in which World Vision Tanzania focuses on empowering the poor.

---

6. Tim Chester, ed., *Justice, Mercy and Humility: Integral Mission and the Poor* (Carlisle, UK, and Waynesboro, Ga.: Paternoster Press, 2002), 19.

7. Ibid., 20.

8. Bryant L. Myers, *Walking with the Poor: Principles and Practices of Transformational Development* (Maryknoll, N.Y.: Orbis Books, 1999), 58.

We Can Do Something

Typically, a community welcomes a development NGO with hospitality and presents it with a list of things the community would like done. Insisting on a discussion focusing on what has worked and on when and how the community has been successful in the past is very helpful in getting past the initial view of the NGO as the giver of good things. Through community meetings and focus groups, World Vision Tanzania works with the community using an appreciative framework to hear the community's answers to questions like the following:

- What life-giving, life-enhancing forces do you have in your community? What gives you the energy and power to change and to cope with adversity?
- Thinking back on the last one hundred years of your community, what has happened that you are proud of, that makes you feel you have been successful?
- What are your best religious and cultural practices? Those that make you feel good about your culture? That have helped you when times were tough?
- What do you value that makes you feel good about yourselves?
- What in your geographical area and in your local political and economic systems has helped you do things you are proud of?
- What skills or resources have enabled you to do things your children will remember you for having done?
- How have your relationships, both within and without the community, worked for you and helped you do things that you believe were good for the community?

The net result of such an inquiry is often spectacular. The laundry list of problems the community would like the NGO to fix is lost in the enthusiasm of describing what is already working. The community comes to view its past and itself in a new light. We do know things. We do have resources. We have a lot to be proud of. We are already on the journey. God has been good to us. We can do something.[a]

_____

a. Myers, *Walking with the Poor*, 178–79.

In addition to ethical considerations there are strong practical arguments in favor of "empowering" the poor, building local ownership, and "helping the poor to help themselves." Studies across countries and cultures have found that poverty reduction efforts that involve the leadership of impoverished women and men and develop their organizational capacities are, by and large, more cost effective, longer lasting, more successful, and more valued by the community for years to come.

Obviously "empowerment" of each and every individual is not always directly appropriate, because included among impoverished communities are infants, the elderly, those with physical and mental disabilities, or people passing through difficult points of life. But it often comes in indirectly. Goal 4 of the MDGs aims to reduce child mortality by two-thirds. What is less obvious is the fact that the poor can be architects of this change. One of the best ways to reduce child mortality is by educating and empowering young mothers so that they know how to prevent dehydration and common infections and provide better nutrition and hygiene for their little ones.

MDGs

Goal 4: Reduce child mortality

Specifically, the target is to reduce by two-thirds, between 1990 and 2015, the number of children who die before their fifth birthday. At present one small life slips away every three seconds — 11 million children a year. For developing countries on average, under-five child mortality was measured at roughly 80 deaths per 1,000 in 1990. The goal is to lower this by two-thirds by 2015 to roughly 28 deaths per 1,000. In high-income countries there are 7 deaths per 1000.

Why do children die?

Seventy percent of the child deaths before age five could have been prevented. Most children die of these causes: malnutrition, diarrhea, measles, malaria, and acute respiratory infections, as well as HIV/AIDS. Over one in five child deaths occur during the first week of life, mostly due to mothers' malnutrition; 40 percent are in the first month, and 70 percent in the first year. Progress in other MDGs — particularly girls' and women's education and safe water — are needed to meet this MDG, demonstrating again the interconnectedness of the goals.

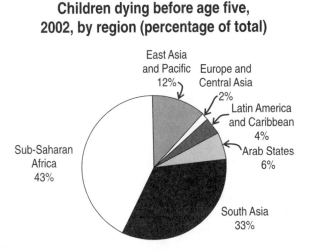

Children dying before age five, 2002, by region (percentage of total)

Source: World Bank, *World Development Indicators 2004* (Washington, D.C.).

How are we doing so far?

Despite the fact that many deaths could be prevented by relatively straight-forward and low-cost interventions, the prospects of realizing this particular MDG are gravely low. *Only 15–20 percent of poor countries are on track to reduce child mortality by two-thirds.* Of the regions of the world, northern Africa, Latin America, and Southeast Asia are nearly on track. Other areas need to accelerate their progress.

QUESTION FOR DISCUSSION

◆ Given that the means to save children's lives are simple and low cost, it seems a travesty that we are so far off track in meeting this goal. What role might the churches have in catalyzing action to empower women and communities, and get us back on track?

Why is it important for church members in the West to know about the importance of empowerment? Part of the reason for explaining this is to help those who are advocating poverty reduction understand some of the mechanisms by which poverty can be effectively reduced. But it may also affect how we act as givers, as the following story demonstrates.

A church's women's group in the US established a relationship with a church in Sub-Saharan Africa. They exchanged letters and were getting to know one another. The relationship had been catalyzed by a church mission agency. Then one of the letters from Africa mentioned a need for garden hoes. Bursting with generosity and excitement at the new relationship, and without consulting the agency or partner church, the church ladies procured a dozen new garden hoes and prepared to send them to the African church. At this point the mission agency intervened, arguing that this action was inappropriate — that the hoes might not be strong enough, that hoes could be bought more cheaply in the community, and that it would be better to return the hoes and send the funds across directly. One of the women related this story years after it had occurred. She still seemed crestfallen by the experience, and bitter that the mission agency had rejected her well-intentioned generosity. She and the group also felt accused of imposing — but they hadn't intended to. The experience had left her unsettled, disappointed, and not willing to try again. It is precisely these kinds of miscommunications — with mission agencies and also with partners — which are frequent and which take many forms, that can be prevented if people who start to become involved are adequately informed and communicate well and often with their counterparts.

Other dimensions of impoverishment and flourishing

When all is said and done, though, Jesus' words to the Tempter remain true: we do not live by bread alone. Just as we see how beloved the impoverished are to God, so too we must acknowledge, in the next breath, that poverty is only one aspect of life and, as the case of the contented grandmother referred to earlier in this chapter highlights, does not define a person. For example, the physical "health-related" MDGs try to prevent the most common causes of tragic and premature death. Yet longevity — although important and worthwhile for its own sake — is not alone sufficient for fulfillment.

Clearly, people flourish in different ways. Often people will recognize many kinds of poverty — some people are lonely, others overworked, others stressed, others oppressed by a dominant figure in their lives, and so on. Similarly we are also fulfilled in different ways and to different extents — by enjoying life itself, by having knowledge and understanding, by meaningful work and play, through human relationships, through a sense of serenity and inner peace, by deliberating and considering many decisions, and by a relationship with God.[9] Recognizing the many ways in which we can be both poor and fulfilled helps us to understand both our own situation and that of others more fully.

Recognizing the deep and liberating, yet limited, contribution that poverty alleviation can make is important for a number of reasons. One is that poverty reduction is usually regarded as decisively "good" rather than ethically ambiguous. And it is. Yet material comforts can also divert one from God and from true fulfillment. Liberation from impoverishment may enslave in other ways. Indeed many religious and cultural groups have actively resisted "development" activities. They do not oppose the reduction of poverty, but rather the "godless" materialism and selfish individualism that poverty reduction activities sometimes introduce. Keeping in mind the rich dimensions of fulfillment helps Christians working in or alongside impoverished communities think through these tensions and critically scrutinize the values our well-intentioned activities may inadvertently introduce.

The blessedness of the poor

Is poverty abysmal or blessed? One of the most famous lines in the Gospels is Jesus' beatitude: "Blessed are you who are poor, for yours is the kingdom of God" (Luke 6:20). In Matthew's Sermon on the Mount the term is "poor in spirit" (Matthew 5:3). Through the ages, Christians have been puzzled by what Jesus meant.

Many people act as if death is the worst thing that can happen to one, and pain the most tragic, but they are not. More to be feared are lovelessness, apathy, self-centeredness, or dread. But in our society, so often it seems that what we fear most of all is impoverishment and its companions: exclusion, ridicule, stigma, coercion, or early death. Poverty in spirit may refer to the characteristics in which people — whether they are materially deprived or not — do not rely on material provisions for their security and sense of self. The spiritually poor may be more "totally at the disposition of the Lord."[10] Dealing with harsh conditions of impoverishment sometimes creates a kind of intimacy with one's own limits that deepens the soul. It can even create joy. Kahlil Gibran's phrase is often quoted because it is often found to resonate with people's experience: "The deeper sorrow has carved into your being, the more joy you

---

9. Germain Grisez, Joseph Boyle, and John Finnis, "Practical Principles, Moral Truths, Ultimate Ends," *American Journal of Jurisprudence* 32 (1987): 99–151, with slight modifications to terminology.

10. Gustavo Gutiérrez, *A Theology of Liberation* (Maryknoll, N.Y.: Orbis Books, 1973), 263.

can contain."[11] So the poor in spirit are "blessed" or happy — and this blessedness has a stable core that neither ridicule nor penury can rock.

Another interpretation, mentioned in chapter 3, is that the deprived are especially loved by God. As Mary's Magnificat has reminded Christians through the ages:

> [The Lord] has brought down the powerful from
>   their thrones,
> and lifted up the lowly;
> he has filled the hungry with good things,
> and sent the rich away empty. (Luke 1:52–53)

Travelers are often quite surprised by one form of blessedness, which is hospitality. The most common "moving story" that people tell of their trips to a developing country is the amazement and shame they feel when someone who has a great deal less than they do cooks them a special meal or gives them gifts. Travelers are taken aback partly by embarrassment that people who have so much less are so generous to them, as strangers. Partly too, they are awed by those people who live in conditions that we dread so deeply, and yet rise above their circumstances to be happy or loving or fulfilled or devout.

Voluntary and involuntary poverty are interconnected. For there is a paradox housed in between the two paths of the Christian ethic: "If any want to become my followers, let them deny themselves and take up their cross and follow me" (Matthew 16:24) and Matthew's teaching discussed in chapter 3 which condemns those who see but do not help the hungry, naked, and imprisoned. On the one hand, true "liberation" is found by voluntarily renouncing the things of this world, by accepting real suffering and utter dependence on God. For instance, Christians have often chosen to give up their possessions and to embrace poverty as a path to spiritual intimacy. In the fourth century, Anthony of Egypt fled to the desert and lived an ascetic life of prayer and voluntary poverty. Many others followed suit, for example the thirteenth-century saint Francis of Assisi, who renounced his family's wealth and dramatically and symbolically stripped himself naked in front of his bishop! His companion and counterpart, Clare, who founded the order of Poor Clares, likewise followed an ascetic life. Dorothy Day, the founder of the Catholic Worker movement, balanced voluntary poverty with service. The voluntary poverty of monks, nuns, and other Christians remains a powerful reminder of the spiritual liberation this state of life can bring.

---

11. Kahlil Gibran, *The Prophet* (New York: Knopf, 1923), 36.

Yet, on the other hand, liberation is also to be found in the good things of this life, in being freed from poverty, oppression, and disease; in becoming educated and empowered and fulfilled; in working alongside God for the coming of God's reign.

Filling out our analysis of poverty does not create any ethical quandary with respect to the MDGs. Wealthy Christians (among others) are obliged to enable others to avoid involuntary extreme poverty. All persons, rich and poor, must also consider whether or not to seek out and embrace poverty voluntarily at a personal level. Finally all persons, including the impoverished, are to seek spiritual blessedness and union with God in any state of life — and in this regard the materially poor may be ahead of others.

Two final points need to be made to counter a sentimental understanding of poverty to which people sometimes appeal. First, poverty is not sanctity. It goes along with all moods. Depravity and viciousness are found among all; so too gentleness and prayerfulness. Second, extreme poverty — upon which this book focuses — is distinct from the elegant simplicity of life that many seek. It is harsh, burdensome, and not generally desirable. Yet those who live in these conditions at times flourish with amazing generosity, hospitality, and faith, and challenge our own overdependence upon material comforts and our own fear of material impoverishment. We have much to learn from them. As the theologian Dorothee Soelle writes, "From the poor of Latin America I learn their hope, their toughness, their anger, and their patience. I learn a better theology in which God is not Lord-over-us but Strength-in-us."[12]

In conclusion, many Christians and church groups seem hesitant to acknowledge the resilience, fallibility, and leadership of impoverished people and communities. It would seem to complicate the task of poverty reduction. Instead, many groups working with the poor make donors feel like saintly and powerful benefactors (and the donors, to their slight discredit, respond). The impoverished are described as victims. Maybe such groups think that the only way to encourage Christians to give generously is to appeal to their ego and sense of self-importance. This chapter instead suggests that Christians acknowledge the materially poor as equals — which before God they are — and build up relationships that empower them to be the architects of change. Christians face a genuine possibility to support a historical change in the lives of the impoverished,

12. Dorothee Soelle, *Celebrating Resistance: The Way of the Cross in Latin America* (London: Mowbray-Cassell, 1993), 95.

and they needn't be duped or sweet-talked into doing so. The plain truth is exciting enough.

⁇ QUESTION FOR DISCUSSION

Two visitors came to a desert village that had just dug a well and was starting its first girls' school. One of the visitors was a journalist from the capital city. After talking with a group of women about the changes in their village, the journalist asked the women if they knew the name of their prime minister. They did not. She asked if they had been to a market town less than twenty-five miles away any time in their lives. They had not. The journalist then asked the women how they viewed her and her companion. "We are dirty; we work in the sand," one woman observed. "You are clean. And you will leave when you wish."

Think of what you have access to that the poor do not. You may think of the education, the entertainment, the food, the cleanliness, the electronic and computer resources, the diversity of music, the ability to travel, or many other things.

Now imagine you are standing in front of God beside the poorest person you know. The person beside you has as direct an access to God's ear and attention and love as you do. In this you are both equal. The person beside you can interrupt you, accuse you, admire you, can comfort you. How does that make you feel about the poor person? How does that make you feel about God, that God gives them equal time and attention as God gives you? How does that make you feel about yourself? If you knew that this meeting would occur in one year's time, what would you do differently now?

ACTION 4:
CONNECT WITH THE IMPOVERISHED

This action asks you to consider connecting with the impoverished and also building up the body of Christ by engaging with people of faith around the world.

Why this is strategic

A resident of Manhattan can be in Mumbai in seventeen hours, a Londoner in fewer than ten. In the past decade or so, long-distance international travel has become considerably faster, more affordable, and highly popular. It is now a common feature of business life and leisure.

A journey can alter the heart forever; travel can broaden the mind. It may seem in an era of twenty-four-hour news channels, live satellite remote broadcasts, and keyhole satellite pictures that nothing is hidden from us anymore. We can see everything. And yet we live among hidden worlds, invisible because we never look at them. The lives of whole communities of people are shielded from us. When we step into these other places, we may be given a precious gift: a moment or a series of moments that can galvanize and sustain our commitment long after we return home. We can, if you like, begin to see the bigger picture, the rich diversity of the world God has created — and our role in it. Furthermore, as Christians it enhances our understanding of the body of Christ — a worldwide fellowship of faith that could potentially unite us with billions of others, and not only fellow members of our local church.

The value of firsthand experience

Newspapers, books, television, and the Internet can all provide information on global poverty. Yet the learning experiences that come to us through the media are, by definition, mediated experiences. Firsthand experiences of poverty — with sounds and smells — can help take us beyond the previous limits of our empathy. A learning journey can create genuine connections and help to pull us out of our observer status and into our fully connected humanity.

Such is the value of relating to the poor in this way that development agencies are increasingly using what are termed "immersions," placements where their senior staff are sent to live in impoverished communities and learn for themselves about the lives of the people their organizations seek to empower. Margarit M. W. Suárez, a Cuban American theologian, described the impact of a sudden and rather painful stint in rural Cuba on her research: "I needed to be dislocated in order to appreciate the dislocation of the people around me.... I hadn't taken the time to sit and reflect, to be vulnerable, and had not fully appreciated the grace of the community, which made it bearable."[13]

Encounters of this kind are not only learning experiences, they build relationships. One of the greatest joys of being part of a community of faith is to celebrate that faith with others — to know that you love and serve the same God, even if you do not speak the same language or share the same culture. Mission trips and other international connections provide opportunities for forging new and diverse relationships with fellow

---

13. Margarit M. W. Suárez, "Across the Kitchen Table: Cuban Women Pastors," in *Gender, Ethnicity, and Religion: Views from the Other Side,* ed. Rosemary Radford Ruether (Minneapolis: Fortress Press, 2002), 190.

Christians overseas, which can be mutually enriching, as can encounters with those of other faiths.

Following are three practical ways to connect with others.

1. Voluntary service

A number of development organizations rely on volunteers who are willing to work in deprived parts of the world, particularly people who have skills that are in short supply, such as in medicine, engineering, and teaching. There is enormous diversity in the type, length, and location of these volunteer programs. Recognizing that not everyone can simply take off for six months or a year, many initiatives have much briefer terms, some as short as two weeks.

With increasing numbers of students in the US and UK taking a gap year before or during university, there are growing opportunities for young people to do voluntary work overseas; in fact, many universities actively encourage this. If there are young people in your church interested in voluntary work overseas, why not support and sponsor them?

The hardest part is getting started. It's easiest to begin by using online databases and search engines that allow you to match your interests and abilities with appropriate programs. Some useful Web sites are listed beginning on page 104. Once you have narrowed your search, most agencies will have more complete information on their own Web sites. You might have to e-mail three or four groups until you finalize a placement. Remember not to overlook your church and church-based organizations, as many run volunteer programs.

2. Business and tourism

Successful and ethical experiential travel demands that travelers are not simply voyeurs of the images of poverty. Still, there is considerable merit in recognizing that the opportunity to connect with the impoverished may exist in places where you travel.

Willis Jenkins, a Fellow at the Institute for Practical Ethics and Public Life at the University of Virginia, suggests that ordinary business or leisure travel can provide opportunities to "step outside the bubble" to interact in a local market, walk through a village, or eat in a local home. He also recommends that travelers plan ahead and budget a day to volunteer or look up a local NGO to learn about their work — something that again usually takes only a few e-mails to set up. In this way you can connect briefly with the impoverished in their daily lives and be part of their lives — and they of yours — at that moment.

An alternative approach is to take part in an organized holiday with an ethical slant. For instance, Traidcraft, a leading supplier of Fair Trade products in the UK, organizes "People to People Tours," holidays that include visits to the producers of Fair Trade products in developing countries. There is something profoundly moving when a Western consumer can meet — and thank — a person from a developing country for the goods that he or she enjoys. Similarly, a number of churches organize holidays in developing countries, offering the mutual opportunity for those from different societies to share in fellowship and worship.

Firsthand encounters of this kind are not suitable for everyone. It is critical to understand your own personal limits, both physical and psychological, and to be aware of safety issues. If for whatever reason such a journey is not feasible, you can still enrich your understanding by connecting with someone who has undertaken such a trip. Better still, you can invite them to speak to your church or to a group of your friends. Not all epiphanies involve airplanes, and not all journeys require passports.

3. Companion relationships/twinning programs

An increasingly popular way of connecting with others is through church-to-church relationships. In the Church of England and in the Episcopal Church in the United States, for example, many dioceses have well-established links with Anglican dioceses in developing countries. These links provide an ongoing relationship as well as opportunities for exchanges of church members or clergy, letter writing, and practical projects — and periodic parish visits. What visiting church groups most often say is that they are overwhelmed by the hospitality they receive and are uplifted by the vibrancy of the worship in which they take part. For instance, a church in the Diocese of Oxford in the UK is currently raising money for a new church room, but as part of the same "Living Rooms" project it is also raising funds to build an HIV/AIDS center in the link diocese of Kimberley and Kuruman in South Africa. The Diocese of Massachusetts gives 0.7 percent of diocesan income to a very active Jubilee program that supports HIV/AIDS projects in Africa, which members of the diocese can and do visit. Encounters of this kind are mutually enriching and a practical expression of "building up the body of Christ."

Web sites for visiting and volunteering

US

Bridges to Community: *www.bridgestocommunity.org/*

Cross-Cultural Solutions: *www.crossculturalsolutions.org*

International Volunteer Programs Association: *www.volunteerinternational.org*

United States Peace Corps: *www.peacecorps.gov*

UN Volunteers for Peace and Development: *www.unv.org*

The International Ecotourism Society: *www.ecotourism.org/*

UK

Church Mission Society: *www.cms-uk.org*. (Look for Praxis holidays).

Traidcraft: *www.traidcraft.co.uk*.

United Society for the Propagation of the Gospel: *www.uspg.org.uk*

Voluntary Service Overseas: *www.vso.org.uk*

Volunteering England: *www.volunteering.org.uk*

Church sites on overseas volunteer and travel opportunities:

Baptist: *http://going.imb.org/*

Catholic: *www.catholicrelief.org/about_us/careers/volunteer_ opportunities/index.cfm*

Episcopalian: *www.episcopalchurch.org/30703_1700_ENG_ HTM.htm?menu=menu7941*

Mennonite: *www.mcc.org/servicetree/index.html*

These are only a very few! Please check out your own church's Web site.

Other

World Service Enquiry: *www.wse.org.uk*. This is a site in the UK that is also useful for Americans interested in working or visiting overseas.

www.responsibletravel.com. Backed by Anita Roddick of the Body Shop, this site offers only holidays that have been screened on environmental, social, and economic grounds.

www.sewaacademy.org/training/tr_edp.htm. In India the Self-Employed Women's Association runs exposure programs for foreign professionals, including parliamentarians and senior staff of the World Bank.

Information about immersions can be found at:
   www.livelihoods.org/lessons/docs/IMMERSION2.pdf
   and *www.ids.ac.uk/bookshop/briefs/PB22.pdf*.

5

Where Is God
When People Suffer?

Sex for Food

Pemba, a town in the southern Monze region of Zambia, has fewer than five thousand inhabitants.... As I was having a drink at a grocery near the main road, I saw two boys and a girl between six and thirteen years old picking up kernels of maize. The children told me that their mother sent them to pick the grain so that they could grind it into "mealie meal" and make *nsima* (a thick local porridge). The children did this often.

I asked them to show me where their mother was. We found her at home lying on a reed mat. After I explained who I was, she agreed to have a conversation. When I asked her what she did for a living, she looked at me for some time then looked down and sighed.

"My husband was discharged in 1994," she began. "He was our sole bread-winner. I was a full-time housewife and mother. I thought I would never have to earn an income. Food was never a problem and everything was well with us. We managed well with my husband's income.

"Things changed after my husband left the army. He did not receive his benefits for two years, which meant the family had no income. My husband couldn't cope and died of depression in 1997. Though his benefits came before he died, most of the money went to repay the debts we had accumulated. We experienced serious food shortages. We often went without a good meal for several days. My children always wore hungry and sad faces. I tried to sell vegetables but everyone else sold vegetables, too. Whatever I sold didn't bring in much.

"I had no choice but to send my children to beg in town and glean the maize that dropped from trucks passing along the road. But this was no solution. I had to find food for my family."

She paused, looked down with a clenched fist, hit her chest, and said, "Against my own will, against my faith, I became a walker. I slept with men for money. At first it tormented me and I found it extremely hard to understand. Today I do it with less difficulty."

"Do not ask me about sexually transmitted diseases," she said. "I may or may not be a carrier. But as long as I can afford a meal for my family, I am happy. I know that one day I will die of AIDS," she said, on the verge of tears. "But I can tell you that I find hunger more deadly than AIDS. AIDS kills in years. But hunger kills within days."

I had few words to say except to thank her for her time. She never mentioned school, health, entertainment, or clothing...only food. I realized that when you have no food, you have no choice.

—Joseph Kalungu Sampa, assistant coordinator of the
Structural Adjustment Policy Monitoring Project in Lusaka
and a participant in Bread for the World Institute's
Africa Writers' Project. Used with permission.

How can there be a God of love when there is so much suffering in the world? This question has been asked time and time down the ages. It refuses to go away. It is a question asked in despair by those who witnessed the horrors of the Holocaust and the genocides in Sudan, Rwanda, Kosovo, and Sierra Leone. It is a question asked by those who confront the carnage of warfare. It is a question that surfaces when we read stories like the one of the Zambian woman above. It is a question asked by many appalled by the devastation of the 2004 tsunami in the Indian Ocean or bombings in London. It is a question that millions of devout and faithful people have wrestled with as they have nursed a relative or friend dying of AIDS or cancer. It is a question we may ask out of personal experience. It is a question that has destroyed the faith of some and unsettled the faith of many.

It is also a question that comes to mind when we focus our attention on the Millennium Development Goals. For what lies behind the statistics of HIV infection, income levels, illness, water supplies, and literacy rates are billions of stories of hardship, vulnerability, and tragedy — and of hard-heartedness, selfishness, oversight, and intransigence on the part of others. Statistics cannot possibly quantify the extent of this suffering; only God knows the anguish that extreme poverty and disease cause. And as the previous chapter pointed out, recognition of the resilience, wisdom, and joy of some who live in extreme poverty must stand alongside an acknowledgment of their hardship.

But the question does not go away. It is asked by those engaged in poverty reduction, whose work brings home the reality of suffering. The more we focus our attention on poverty, the more we realize its consequences and potential to break lives. The more we think about disease, the more we see forces at work destroying families, communities, and human potential. The section below, for example, gives us an update of the HIV/AIDS pandemic.

MDGs

Goal 6: Combat HIV/AIDS, malaria, and other diseases

We are taking this goal out of order (the previous chapter addressed Goal 4) — but then AIDS came upon us out of order. It interrupted us. It deserves our attention. We will discuss Goal 5 in chapter 7.

Specifically, the target is to have halted by 2015, and begun to reverse, the spread of HIV/AIDS and the incidence of malaria and other major diseases.

In 2003, 3 million people died of HIV/AIDS, and 5 million were newly infected. About 1.8 million people died of tuberculosis in 2003, and about 1 million people died of malaria — the other main infectious diseases upon which this goal focuses. HIV/AIDS is the leading cause of death among adults aged 15–59 worldwide. This section focuses upon the HIV/AIDS pandemic, which causes untold suffering to families, communities, and friends, and throws countries into economic as well as social crises. When HIV/AIDS prevalence reaches 8 percent, as in thirteen African countries, national economic growth slows by about 1 percent.

The *World Health Report 2004* contains the following update about HIV/AIDS:

- Approximately 40 million people are now living with HIV/AIDS (34–46 million); 20 million people have already perished from it.

- Of these 40 million people, 27 million of them live in Sub-Saharan Africa, where the crisis is at its most intense.

- Globally, most HIV is spread by unprotected sexual intercourse between men and women.

- In the absence of diagnosis and treatment, people live with HIV for nine to eleven years on average before developing the full AIDS infection.

- Today, about one in twelve African adults has HIV/AIDS, and about 30 percent of people living with HIV/AIDS worldwide live in southern Africa, an area that is home to just 2 percent of the world's population.

- In Sub-Saharan Africa women aged 15–24 are 2.5 times as likely to be infected as are men, as they are forced into unequal sexual relationships and may be unable to negotiate safe sex. Worldwide 59 percent of the people living with HIV/AIDS are women.

* The world holds 14 million HIV/AIDS orphans, most of them living in Africa. By 2010, estimates are that up to one-quarter of Sub-Saharan Africa's children will be orphans.

* The Caribbean has the second highest HIV/AIDS prevalence in the world after Sub-Saharan Africa, with 2–3 percent of the adults being infected.

* At present, almost 6 million people in developing countries need antiretroviral therapy (which reduces death rates by 80 percent), but only 400,000 received it in 2003.

Adults and children living with HIV/AIDS, by region

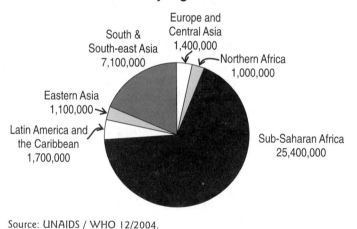

Source: UNAIDS / WHO 12/2004.

How are we doing so far?

The answer is, badly. The HIV/AIDS pandemic is not at all contained in Sub-Saharan Africa, where pregnant women 15 to 24 years of age display infection rates of 18 to 39 percent, and preventive measures, education, and treatment are all urgently needed.

Progress is possible, and many countries have put forward the concerted effort required to contain the HIV/AIDS pandemic. For example in Lusaka, Zambia, HIV prevalence among adolescents aged 15–19 decreased from 28 percent to 15 percent in just five years. A vigorous program providing life skills education and health services for teenagers helped to increase condom use and decrease the number of sexual partners. But there is much to do. Because churches teach about human sexuality, relationships, and procreation, and because Christians are themselves deeply affected by HIV/AIDS, churches have a disproportionate ability to affect this pandemic: to prevent it by good knowledge and teaching, and to challenge the stigma to which HIV-positive people are often subjected.

QUESTION FOR DISCUSSION

◆ This chapter began with the story of a mother who is likely going to perish of HIV/AIDS, and the section above gives further information about the HIV/AIDS crisis. What issues do these raise for you? Where, for you, is God in their suffering?

Our responses to suffering differ. Some of us are driven to our knees to call on God, for we perceive that dealing with the situation is beyond our capability. We do what we can, praying that the rest will be dealt with in God's own good way and time. For others, the thirst for justice may make us question why, if there is a God of love, should God allow such suffering to take place — after all, it seems so unfair, so *un*just? Many of those who suffer are innocent, the victims of circumstance. Their plight may call us to question whether we are working alongside God for justice, or whether are we working to make right those awful things God seems to allow or even inflict upon humanity. It is not uncommon to discover people working for humanitarian organizations who did so at first because of religious belief, but who have since lost their faith in a loving God.

Others have their faith severely shaken. This was the experience of Michael Taylor, the former director of Christian Aid, the most prominent church-based relief and development agency in the UK, who through his travels and firsthand contact with those living in poverty began to realize "that human suffering was not an aberration but the norm."[1] For Taylor, this led to a crisis of faith: "My Christianity had coped with suffering. But this sudden and sobering awareness of it as 'normal' made the issue far more pressing, as personal tragedy often does for others,

---

1. Michael Taylor, *Poverty and Christianity: Reflections at the Interface between Faith and Experience* (London: SCM Press, 2000), 10.

and made me wonder how Christianity could cope with it all or possibly defend it."[2]

When our heart moves us to question our faith in this way, we must put our mind to the problem. When we do, we will be in good company, as many have done so down the ages, including Job, who protested to God about his own suffering and sure death twenty-five hundred years ago:

> I cry to you and you do not answer me;
> I stand, and you merely look at me.
> (Job 30:20)

Perhaps such questions are troubling you as you read this book. After all, by now you will have a good idea of the extent of global poverty, and a sense of the personal tragedies that lie behind the statistics, and particularly the tragedy of those with HIV/AIDS, including children and orphans. The question of where God is when people suffer is worthy of attention and reflection.

Not that this chapter will offer a satisfactory explanation, for nobody has managed to reconcile suffering with a God of love in a way that stops the question from recurring. Furthermore, theological explanations may not be helpful. As Dorothee Soelle comments, "Theologians have an intolerable passion for explaining and speaking when silence would be appropriate."[3] In the following pages you will read some of the arguments that have been put forward through history in an effort to link our experience of suffering to our belief in a loving God. You may find some of the explanations compelling, and yet you may find some disturbing or wrong. We are not trying to offer a conclusion or to endorse one particular point of view, but rather to provide material for your own reflections.

?? QUESTION FOR DISCUSSION

◆ How has your faith been affected by your own personal experience of suffering — whether your own or others'?

---

2. Ibid., 11–12.
3. Dorothee Soelle, *Suffering*, trans. Everett Kalin (Philadelphia: Fortress Press, 1975), 19.

The Overwhelming Goodness of God

Many or most of the arguments that try to reconcile God and suffering address this question: if God is good, why does God allow such suffering? The problem with these arguments is that, because we cannot find a good justification for suffering, we end up "attributing perverse motives to God" — for example, that God causes suffering to teach people to be virtuous.[4]

So we begin with a different account. In a powerful book on "horrendous evil," the priest and philosopher Marilyn McCord Adams argues that a better way of approaching the topic of suffering is to ask another question: how is God good to people who suffer and experience horrendous evil? She does not minimize extreme suffering. The focus of her reflections is the kind of evil that is so horrendous that it could and may ruin a person's earthly life, and the focus of her response is God's willingness through the incarnation and crucifixion of Jesus to identify with all victims and perpetrators. But she argues that human victims will enjoy heavenly beatitude — the land of milk and honey, the eternal banquet, rejoicing in God's presence — after this life. Then they will be overwhelmed by the goodness of God. While suffering is by no means necessary for them to enjoy God, in looking back across their lives, people who have suffered a great deal will be able to identify with some aspects of God, to recognize God's goodness toward them not through — but during — those experiences.[5]

Suffering and soul-making

An alternative approach to suffering — at least the nonhorrendous kind — is to ask whether it can serve any useful purpose. This is what the philosopher of religion John Hick attempted in his book *Evil and the God of Love*. He imagines what our world would be like if God intervened so that no wrong action on the part of humans could ever have bad effects. It would be a world where murder weapons would be made harmless, a world where road accidents would leave those involved unharmed, and a world where the law of gravity would be suspended if someone fell from a building. At first, this sort of utopian world may seem an attractive option. But Hick goes on to make this point:

> The daunting fact that emerges is that in such a world moral qualities would no longer have any point or value. There would be

---

4. Ibid., 156.
5. Marilyn McCord Adams, *Horrendous Evils and the Goodness of God* (Ithaca, N.Y.: Cornell University Press, 1999).

nothing wrong with stealing, because no one could ever lose anything by it; there would be no such crime as murder, because no
one could ever be killed. ... If to act wrongly means, basically, to
harm someone, there would be no way in which anyone could in-
jure anyone else, but there would also be no way in which anyone
could benefit anyone else, since there would be no possibility of any
lack or danger. It would be a world without need for the virtues of
self-sacrifice, care for others, devotion to the public good, courage,
perseverance, skill, or honesty. It would indeed be a world in which
such qualities, having no function to perform, would never come
into existence.[6]

So, according to Hick, in a world in which God intervened to prevent
suffering, our sense of morality would be blunted or extinguished, as all
bad actions would be put right by God. We would never develop virtuous behavior, because there would be no need to be virtuous. Climbing
Mount Everest would no longer require courage, because it would not be
dangerous. Truthfulness would be redundant, as telling lies could never
have harmful consequences. Most important of all, our capacity to love
would diminish, because at its most profound level love is about caring
for others and sharing their burdens. In a world without suffering there
would be no opportunity to express love in this way.

We might have been tempted to think of God's love in terms of pro-
tection — of God wanting to shield us from all harm or danger. This is a
very natural thing to do, and it may be something that we pray for. After
all, as loving parents we will try to protect our children from harm. So
if God is our loving Creator, surely God would do the same for us?

If we take this analogy a little further, however, Hick argues that
something is amiss. Overprotective parents can do all sorts of damage
to their children's development. A child must be allowed to fall off a
bicycle if she is to learn to ride it. Overprotected children may never learn
how to enjoy life to the full or cope with the pressures of adulthood.
Overprotective behavior toward our children may be far from loving,
for if the purpose of love is to care for others in ways that nurture, then
surely we must equip them to navigate the real world. Loving parents
allow their children to be exposed to risks and dangers, but in a careful
and caring way, so that they gradually learn to make the most of their
lives and gain the ability to cope by themselves.

Hick tries to extend this analogy to what he understands by the "God
of love." In the world in which we live — in the world that God has

6. John Hick, *Evil and the God of Love* (London: Fontana, 1968), 360–61.

created — God's love for us is not experienced in ways that shield and protect us from suffering, as if God were an overprotective parent. Instead, we may experience God's love as we would the love of a wise parent or our closest friend — as the love of someone who is with us in good times and bad, and when we suffer, being there to share our burden.

This argument might work well if suffering was always a learning device, like falling off of a bicycle, or a passing stage, like sore muscles. But not all suffering is obviously constructive, or virtue creating. Some is what McCord Adams calls "horrendous." Consider the poverty campaigner and musician Bob Geldof's description of children dying in northern Ethiopia: "These wizened old men and women aged two or three died about me in a thick stew of foul stench and a pandemonium glut of delirious flies." What does a child learn from this? Geldof's response was not admiration for God's ability to instruct, nor even grief: "Pity was too soft, too, too indulgent.... This was not the happenchance of environment, nor the accident of an indifferent God, this was the malignant hand of humanity laid bare. That anger has lasted 20 years."[7]

While Hick argues that suffering has a purpose in forming people in the image and likeness of God, he freely admits this to be a wholly inadequate explanation for why God should allow horrendous suffering of the type Geldof describes — and many people today endure.

?? QUESTION FOR DISCUSSION

◆ How do you understand the phrase "God of love"? Does Hick's analogy work for you?

Free will

Before we continue, it may be worth pausing to note that any "explanation" for why God allows such suffering will inherently be lacking. We do not and fully cannot know the mind and will of God. How much suffering does God prevent that we never know about? How much of the suffering that does happen is "caused" by God; how much does God "allow"? It is impossible for us to know the answers to these questions, but it doesn't change how important they are to us.

---

7. Bar Council Human Rights Committee Lecture, St. Paul's Cathedral, London, April 20, 2004.

An influential but disputed Christian philosophical defense for the presence of widespread suffering in a world created by a God of love is what is known as the "free will argument." The third-century theologian Origen of Carthage was one of the first people to put forward this line of thinking. The argument runs as follows: Out of love, God has created us as free beings. Out of love, we are not controlled or manipulated by God. God's will for us is that we grow in love and union with God — but in order for that love to grow up truly, God must give us total freedom as to how we live our lives. This freedom includes the freedom to reject God as well as to accept and love God. So we are free to choose what we do or do not do; we are free to make choices for good or for ill; we are free to be cruel, insensitive, and heartless — or saintly — toward others.

Freedom, Origen argued, is God's loving gift to us, yet this freedom brings in its wake the occasions of suffering. The most obvious cost is that we can deliberately choose to abuse this freedom, which will have consequences not only for us but also for those whose lives we affect directly or indirectly. For instance, those who choose to drink and drive knowing its dangers may not only put their own lives and those of their passengers at risk, but also the lives of pedestrians or fellow motorists who use a sidewalk or drive a car.

So according to free will arguments, when we begin to examine suffering we see that so much of it stems from how we use or abuse God's gift of freedom, or how society operates. If we were to apply this argument to the objectives of the MDGs, we might also say that the suffering caused by poverty is also the consequence of how humanity chooses to use its freedom, both deliberately and unintentionally, with the consequence that many are impoverished at the expense of those who live in abundance. The philosophers' God (which may not be the same as a fully Christian conception of God), having given us free will in order that we might learn to love, is therefore not able to prevent the suffering we freely cause.

The omnipotence of God?

While the free will argument takes a position on the nature of God and the world God has created, even if you agree with this argument not all suffering can be explained as a consequence of human free will. There are still natural disasters that cannot be anticipated, there are diseases that are products of the created order. And how can the suffering that is the consequence not of human folly, but of premeditated evil, be explained? God is still a God who not only permits suffering as a consequence of the gift of free will, but who permits suffering that is beyond our control. And so hard as we might try, and as frustrating as it may be, even the most persuasive attempts to make sense of the presence of suffering cannot fully answer the question of why a loving God should allow it.

The dreadful events of the twentieth century — in particular the carnage of the First World War and the Holocaust — have had a profound effect on Judeo-Christian thinking about suffering. One school of thought is that these events have led to "the death of God"; they are proof that a loving God does not exist. Another line of thinking is that God does not deliberately choose not to intervene to prevent suffering, but that God's powers are limited. In other words, God is not — or not yet — omnipotent. The German theologian Jürgen Moltmann writes, "The challenges to faith and the theological difficulties [caused by suffering] arise because people believe that the omnipotence and omnipresent kingdom in which God 'o'er so wondrously reigneth' is already present here and now. That is a fallacy."[8]

For Moltmann, then, that kingdom when God's reign is supreme is yet to come. Such an understanding overcomes at a stroke the contradiction of suffering and a God of love and provides a vacuum in which suffering and evil can exist. It raises all sorts of questions about the nature of God as Creator of the universe. Can it be that God almighty is not yet "all mighty"?

Jesus Christ and suffering

A creedal tenet of the Christian faith is that God incarnate suffered "under Pontius Pilate." Often when we talk of the suffering of Christ we focus on the cross, the fact that Christ suffered an excruciatingly painful and humiliating death. But Jesus would have experienced other traumas, as the Gospels suggest. If Joseph died in his lifetime, Jesus would have suffered bereavement. He wept over the death of his friend Lazarus. Fasting brought at least one experience of physical hunger. He suffered by seeing the anguish of his mother at the crucifixion. In Jesus, God experienced what it is to be a human being and live in a world shaped by suffering.

Another insight that affects the Christian attitude toward suffering is the widely held belief that Christ's suffering was somehow integral to God's plan of salvation for humanity: it is through Christ's death on the cross that God and humans are reconciled. Why Christ's suffering should have this outcome, if that is indeed the case, is another of the great mysteries of the Christian faith. Nevertheless, we understand the

8. Jürgen Moltmann, *God for a Secular Society: The Public Relevance of Theology* (Minneapolis: Fortress Press, 1999), 185.

crucifixion as integral to Christ's resurrection — and hence our hope of salvation.

The focus on Jesus' suffering may provide an important clue to explain an observation that is especially relevant to this book. That is, we might expect that those who are most angry with God, or reject God, would be people who suffer most in our world — including the poor and the oppressed. Yet this is far from the case. Rather, the church is at its most vibrant in many of the world's poorest countries. The faithfulness of the impoverished to God — a faithfulness that God can count on, as God counted on Job — is powerfully expressed by the Brazilian poet Leon Felipe, who wrote in light of "the repeated slum clearances endured by the poor, whose huts of corrugated iron or cardboard are bulldozed":

> We know there is no promised land
> nor any promised stars.
> We know it, Lord, we know it
> and we labor on, with you.
> We know that a thousand more times
> we have to hitch the wagon anew
> and a thousand times
> build our wooden shack
> on the dirt all over again.
> We know that in so doing
> we'll recover neither our costs nor gain profit.
> We know it, Lord, we know it
> and we labor on, with you.
> And we know
> that on this shabby stage,
> a thousand and more thousand times,
> we must play the old tragic-comic play
> without applause or recognition.
> We know it, Lord, we know it
> and we labor on, with you.
> And you know, Lord, that we know it,
> that we all know it, all of us!
> (Where Is the Devil?)
> That today you can make a wager
> with whomever,
> a wager more certain than with Job or with Faust.[9]

---

9. Quoted in Dorothee Soelle, *The Silent Cry: Mysticism and Resistance,* trans. Barbara and Martin Rumscheidt (Minneapolis: Fortress Press, 2001), 135–36.

Perhaps they see in Jesus, the Suffering Servant, someone with whom their lives resonate: born in humble surroundings, a refugee as a child, an artisan, and someone who lived in simplicity with few possessions. Perhaps this is how mothers and fathers view God — a God like them, who suffers with and for his children.

The impoverished may also see themselves as victims of oppressive powers in society. Overcoming "structural sin" and oppression with love was one of the motivations for liberation theology, one of the important schools of thought that grew out of the experiences of the poor and oppressed in Latin America. It has also been a motivating factor in other struggles. Preaching in 1957, as the civil rights movement gained momentum, Martin Luther King gave a powerful description of the synergy between faith and suffering:

> To our most bitter opponents we say, "We shall match your capacity to inflict suffering by our capacity to endure suffering. We shall meet your physical force with soul force. Do to us what you will, and we shall continue to love you. . . . But be ye assured that we will wear you down by our capacity to suffer. One day we shall win freedom, but not only for ourselves. We shall so appeal to your heart and conscience that we shall win you in the process, and our victory will be a double victory" [for] love is the most durable power in the world.[10]

The cloud over Golgotha: Suffering and the absence of God

Some argue that Jesus' suffering on the cross caused him to have a crisis of faith. In Matthew's Gospel we are told that as Christ hung on the cross he cried out the opening words of Psalm 22: "My God, my God, why have you forsaken me?" (Matthew 27:46). The problem is not one of unbelief — for he is praying to God. Rather, it is a crisis because the text can be read as a cry of abandonment, searching for God's response and not yet able to discern it. Surely it is the Father's will not to abandon his Son at this moment?

Jesus' "cry of dereliction" has been echoed by millions of faithful people down the centuries, who seek God — a God they believe in but cannot feel — during suffering.

---

10. Martin Luther King Jr., "Strength to Love," in *A Testament of Hope: The Essential Writings and Speeches of Martin Luther King Jr.* (San Francisco and London: Harper & Row, 1986).

Reflection: Thibault and the Rabbit

Helen Waddell conveyed where God is during suffering in her 1933 novel Peter Abelard. *Abelard — a twelfth-century French theologian best known for his romance with Heloise — explored theological issues others dared not approach. In this story about God and suffering, Abelard and his servant Thibault find a small rabbit caught in a trap making an awful shrieking noise.*

⁓

The rabbit stopped shrieking when they stooped over it, either from exhaustion, or in some last extremity of fear. Thibault held the teeth of the trap apart, and Abelard gathered up the little creature in his hands. It lay for a moment breathing quickly, then in some blind recognition of the kindness that had met it at the last, the small head thrust and nestled against his arm, and it died.

It was the last confiding thrust that broke Abelard's heart. He looked down at the little draggled body, his mouth shaking. "Thibault," he said, "do you think there is a God at all? Whatever has come to me, I earned it. But what did this one do?"

Thibault nodded.

"I know," he said, "Only, I think God is in it too."

Abelard looked up sharply.

"In it? Do you mean that it makes him suffer, the way it does us?"

In the story in the boxes above, the twelfth-century French theologian Peter Abelard argued that God is very present during suffering — even if we do not feel it. Abelard employed an unusual dialogue about the suffering of a forest rabbit, which Abelard and his servant Thibault found caught in a trap and shrieking. They removed the rabbit from the trap; it nuzzled its head into Abelard's arms, then died. Abelard was left to question where God was — because the rabbit did not deserve such a torturous death. Thibault's response was to observe that Calvary — Christ's cross — did not happen at one point in time only. It continues on through history. The story makes a theological point — namely, God is present when people suffer, alongside them. As the theologian John Barton has written:

Again, Thibault nodded.

"Then why doesn't he stop it?"

"I don't know," said Thibault. "Unless it's like the prodigal son. I suppose the father could have kept him at home against his will. But what would have been the use? All this," he stroked the limp body, "is because of us. But all the time God suffers. More than we do."

Abelard looked at him, perplexed. "Thibault, do you mean Calvary?"

Thibault shook his head. "That was only a piece of it — the piece that we saw — in time. Like that." He pointed to a fallen tree beside them, sawn through the middle. "That dark ring there, it goes up and down the whole length of the tree. But you only see it where it is cut across. That is what Christ's life was; the bit of God that we saw. And we think God is like that, because Christ was like that, kind and forgiving sins and healing people. We think God is like that for ever, because it happened once, with Christ. But not the pain. Not the agony at the last. We think that stopped."

Abelard looked at him, the blunt nose and the wide mouth, the honest troubled eyes. He could have knelt before him.

"Then, Thibault," he said slowly, "you think that all this," he looked down at the little quiet body in his arms, "all the pain of the world, was Christ's cross?"

"God's cross," said Thibault. "And it goes on." (pp. 268–70)

The cross is not a momentary lapse or aberration on God's part; it is a single "frame" from an infinite and infinitely consistent story, the story of how God takes all the pain of the world into himself.[11]

Put in contemporary perspective, it would mean that God was present at every scene of suffering you have witnessed, whether far or near and however awful. After the tragedy of September 11 on American soil, after the 2004 tsunami, papers all carried people's stories to this effect. God was present inside the planes, with the people in the World Trade Center towers, the Pentagon, and on a Pennsylvania field on September 11,

11. John Barton, *Love Unknown: Meditations on the Death and Resurrection of Jesus* (London: SPCK, 1990), 23–25.

2001, and in the trains on the Underground and the bus blown apart in London on July 7, 2005, holding the dying, comforting the fearful, urging people to stay home, and offering God's self to those piloting the planes.

QUESTION FOR DISCUSSION

◆ Thibault argued that all of the world's suffering across time is part of "God's cross." What do you think of this viewpoint?

Our responses to suffering

In this chapter we have explored different theological reflections on one of the most recurrent questions of faith: *How can there be a God of love when there is so much suffering in the world?* There is no widely accepted answer. We may or may not find any of the explanations discussed convincing. Some of the explanations may even be wrong. In fact one cannot hold them all at the same time for there are contradictions among them. Yet if suffering causes us to question our faith, then we are in good company. We must look into the problem steadily, and seek spiritual ways to maintain an honest equilibrium in the face of suffering. These reflections on suffering, if we engage in them, may lead us to discover new insights into our own experience and bring us closer to God.

We need also to bear in mind that suffering is a question others will face — perhaps even because of a story we tell, or a special event we organize. Part of the reason to consider such a wide array of reflections is that some of them may not speak to us — but may speak to another, and be a word in time.

ACTION 5:
SPECIAL EVENTS:
MAKE A SONG AND DANCE ABOUT IT

Using the power of music

There are many ways to raise awareness and funds through special events — anything from hunger banquets to bazaars and sales of work. This action suggests organizing a particular kind of special event — a concert — and to channel the power of music and a sense of occasion toward reducing poverty.

Music is strategic because it is a powerful emotional force. It expresses our deepest feelings of joy and of sorrow. It can make us smile, laugh, or cry. Music is also a force of creation in human culture. Music often expresses our search for meaning and is used to probe the "big questions" of life.

Organizing concerts is something the churches are well placed to do, as music is normally an important aspect of church life and the venues often have excellent acoustics. Enthusiasm and common sense rather than expertise are what are required to make a concert work well. In fact, it's often an event organized by novices that proves to be the most successful because of their high level of enthusiasm and desire to make it work. It's also the case that concerts are often most successful in small communities where they are a rarity.

Fund-raising and awareness-raising

Special events such as concerts are an effective way to highlight issues and motivate people, as Live 8 has shown. This aspect makes them particularly useful in the context of talking about poverty and working to promote the MDGs. But it is not enough to listen to a song — people can listen and forget. So what would make a concert powerful and memorable? Here are three guidelines.

First and foremost, it is to **have good music and compelling lyrics**. The singer/songwriter (and Anglican priest) Garth Hewitt, who in a career spanning over thirty years has given many concerts for development agencies, comments that "A song can cut through in a way that a sustained talk may not. The song is the parable and can open people up and put them inside a situation in a way that's very important." Given the emotional power of music and the effectiveness of songs as a means of storytelling, a few well-chosen songs can be an excellent starting point for a campaign or a prelude to a more substantive talk or lecture on an issue.

Second would be to **raise awareness and spark action painlessly.** Concert-goers each have a finite amount of energy for "extra" activities. What could your audience learn to do that would make a difference and fill the need that all of us have to do our bit? Plan something like this: make and hand out flyers with a few pieces of information and something to do (some from this book); host a mailing list for those interested in following up; name the concert after the MDG campaign. The point is to use the concert and the motivation it awakens as a springboard for involvement and action, like the actions set out in this book.

The third would be to provide a concrete way to **use the energy of that evening** — perhaps to raise funds through the concert, or to have postcards or a number to text-message from their cell phones or some other action that people can do then and there that will make a difference. But here again it is important that the action is *strategic*. You could give money to a group that wastes it; you could send postcards that are ill-informed or don't make a difference. Or you could give money in a high-impact way, or send texts that change a policy the next day. The question is not whether you will do a little bit of good, but whether it will be significant, strategic, and give the highest "rate of return" (to use a cold economic phrase) to people's investment of generosity and compassion.

Good music, good information, and a good cause — a powerful concert will include all of these.

What sort of event?

There are many types of musical events and formats that can work. These are a few:

- A concert by a well-known performer who is sympathetic to the cause but plays his or her usual repertoire. The awareness-raising dimension could be through an introduction by a speaker, an interview with someone just before the intermission, and information presented in displays and literature. This event could be advertised as, for instance, "Matilda Major in Concert. In support of the MDGs." The advantage of this type of event is that it should attract a large audience.

- A second approach is to work with lesser-known artists who have expertise in particular aspects of poverty and sing about it. Often organizations can help identify such artists. Concerts of this kind can be very focused and integrated, with the artist not only performing but speaking on the issues with knowledge and insight. Although such a concert may not pull in as large an audience as a concert by a higher-profile artist, this type of event can be particularly powerful for motivating and refreshing people.

- A third approach is to develop a concert around the theme of poverty reduction using local amateur artists, perhaps writing new music for the event. Often local artists have a strong local following. Such an event could be advertised highlighting the theme — for example, "Two Billion Voices — Songs for the Poor, with music by Matilda Minor."

Any of these concerts could be supported by a preconcert event such as an early evening meal with a short presentation on the MDGs.

The key points to consider when putting on concerts are:

- **Decide on your target audience.** This will help you choose the kind of event and the kind of artist to approach. Think also of people who should be invited as special guests, such as church, political, and community leaders.

- **Do your homework on the potential artists.** Listen to CDs, read biographies, reviews, etc. Contact details for artists and/or their management can often be found on CDs or Web sites. There are many thoughtful and sensitive artists who would be delighted to be asked to work to end poverty.

- **Build an enthusiastic team.** The key roles: *chairperson* (to oversee the planning and liaise with the artist/management), *secretary* (to take minutes at planning meetings and do the general administration), *treasurer* (to handle the finances and act as ticket-sales coordinator), *publicity coordinator* (to handle publicity material and contacts with the media), and *event manager* (to oversee the event on the day, including hospitality).

- **Budget carefully from the start.** Budgeting involves making a realistic assessment of all likely costs, a realistic assessment of audience size, setting a sensible ticket price which allows for concessions and group discounts, setting a realistic break even point for ticket sales (a good rule of thumb is to break even on selling 60 percent of tickets). Incidentally, if ticket sales are not going well, it's reassuring to know that about 80 percent of tickets are normally sold in the last two weeks!

- **Look for other sources of funding and help.** Local sponsorship is often available from shops and businesses. A relevant development organization may be willing to copromote a concert. Well-placed shops may also help as ticket outlets. For the private sector, it is charity work and therefore a tax write-off. Supporters of the cause may also be willing to underwrite the event, with their money returned if the event breaks even or makes a profit. Income can also be generated through selling refreshments and programs and by selling advertising space in the programs.

• **Work hard at promotion.** The most effective promotion is through word of mouth, so encouraging church members to get their family and friends to support the event and to sell tickets is a good place to start. Networking with other churches in the locality is important and can also be effective. Posters and flyers can help, but need to be located in places where they will be effective and not put out too early. Local press and radio may provide free publicity, particularly if there is a story linked to the concert — so a well-prepared one-page press release is important.

Budget

How much does it cost to put on a concert? This depends, of course, on many factors. A rough estimate for a performance by a small group of locally based professional musicians might be in the range of $500–$2,000, and the rental of a PA system with a sound engineer might be $300–$700. Flyers and even color posters can be generously supplied for less than $500.

A final point to note is that the success of an awareness-raising event cannot be measured by the size of the audience or revenue. The most successful concert could be one that attracts an audience of fewer than one hundred and results in a financial loss, but which sends people away deeply engaged with the issue and motivated for action. It's good for event organizers — and church committees — to keep this in mind throughout the planning process and after the event, and to see the event as a ministry in and of itself.

6

The Body of Christ

Planting a Tree We Engender Life,
Like Archbishop Romero Did

Poverty reduction and care of the environment are often seen as separate issues. As Ricardo Navarros makes clear, there are very significant connections between them.

The title of this book asks a question, *What can one person do?* The answer is simple. One person can do as much or as little as he or she wants.

When I think of what one person can do, I think of someone who did so much to help the poor and oppressed in my own country, El Salvador. He could have done much more, had his life not been ended by an assassin's bullet. This person I am referring to is Archbishop Oscar Romero.

Archbishop Romero knew what it was like to be poor. He came from a poor peasant family in a remote part of the country. He also knew what it was like to be oppressed, when the military coup of 1979 pushed the country into chaos and the church came under attack. But this quiet priest stood firm, and stood up against the oppressors.

I last spoke to Archbishop Romero on March 23, 1980. The following day, while celebrating a funeral Mass for the mother of a friend, he was shot dead. Just minutes earlier the archbishop preached a sermon in which he said this:

> Those who surrender to the service of the poor through love of Christ will live like the grain of wheat that dies. It only apparently dies. If it were not to die, it would remain a solitary grain. The harvest comes because of the grain that dies. We know that every effort to improve society, above all when society is so full of injustice and sin, is an effort that God blesses; that God wants; that God demands of us.

Archbishop Romero died a quarter of a century ago, a courageous and holy leader. But he lives on with his people like that grain of wheat he spoke about. His voice may have been silenced, but his message has grown in us and is now yielding a harvest!

What he taught those of us who call ourselves Christians is that we have a duty not only to go to church to worship on Sundays, but to fight each and every day against the social problems we face — and there is much work to be done.

To mark the twenty-fifth anniversary of Archbishop Romero's martyrdom, the organization CESTA, of which I am director, is coordinating a national reforestation program. The goal is to plant a million trees within the borders of El Salvador and many more in other countries.

Why did we choose to remember the archbishop by planting trees? First of all, trees can live for many years — for centuries. Last year, when I was in London, I was proud to see the archbishop's statue on the west front of Westminster Abbey, alongside that of Martin Luther King and other great martyrs of the twentieth century. That memorial is in stone and will also last for centuries. But it has no life. It is our hope that people from many countries will plant trees as living memorials.

An important reason for this reforestation project is to honor Archbishop Romero by continuing his work on behalf of the poor. For, as the MDGs recognize, trees are important to local economies. They supply fruit, firewood, shade, and cattle feed, as well as creating natural erosion barriers that can prevent disasters such as landslides. Trees are also the lungs of the planet: they convert carbon dioxide into oxygen, which gives us life. Trees are therefore a vital resource to poor people and their communities. By planting trees we invest in the future of our communities and allow our planet to breathe.

Tree planting is something that anyone can do. Archbishop Romero reached out to everyone with his message — even to his oppressors. In his memory we have invited many groups and organizations to join in, such as churches, schools, community groups, trade unions, businesses, groups of disabled persons, government offices, and NGOs. We especially want children to be involved, as by doing so they can learn about ecology and about Archbishop Romero and watch the trees grow during their lifetime. On each tree there will be a plaque that says appropriately, "Plantando un árbol, sembramos vida, como lo hizo Monseñor Romero" (Planting a tree we engender life, like Archbishop Romero did).

What can one person do? Archbishop Romero has inspired me in my work as an environmentalist. We all have gifts we can use for the service of others in the name of our Creator. It was Archbishop Romero's passionate belief that we should use those gifts — whatever they might be.

— *Ricardo Navarro, director of CESTA and
formerly director of Friends of the Earth International.*

"For just as the body is one and has many members, and all the members of the body, though many, are one body, so it is with Christ. For in the one Spirit we were all baptized into one body" (1 Corinthians 12:12–13). "Let us then pursue what makes for peace and for mutual upbuilding" (Romans 14:19). What does it mean to be the body of Christ? What is it to build up our common life?

The analogy of the people of God as the body of Christ appears most famously in chapter 12 of Paul's First Letter to the Corinthians. Here it reminds the divided church members in Corinth that, like the parts of a body, they too are connected and interdependent: "Now Christ's body is yourselves, each of you with a part to play in the whole" (12:27).

The body of Christ described in 1 Corinthians refers to a particular church at Corinth, but elsewhere it seems to refer to all Christians worldwide (Ephesians 4:12). Theologically, the term can be interpreted to include the non-Christian world, or even the nonhuman world. As God became human — an earthly creature — so God's goodness extends into every living thing on earth, regardless of its faith and form, and through our faith we are called to recognize our interdependence with all of humanity and the rest of God's creation. Whatever the parameters we work within — whether it's the church, humanity, or the created order — the image of the body of Christ brings with it an imperative for action. When one part of the body suffers, the whole of the body is affected, and the rest of the body should respond. As the author of the Letter to the Hebrews wrote, "Keep in mind those who are in prison, as though you were in prison with them; and those who are being badly treated, since you too are in the body" (Hebrews 13:3).

With regard to poverty reduction, at the very least we should share with one another so that no part of the body lies destitute. The Sri Lankan theologian Vinoth Ramachandra points out that the body of Christ is an early analogy for humane and pro-poor globalization:

> Christ is indeed the Head of the Body, but...Christ Himself is found not only in the centre but at the margins of the Body, radically identified with the "least of my brothers and sisters" (Matt. 25:31–46), with whom all the members suffer and rejoice together (1 Cor. 12:26)....Thus...the Gospel collapses spatial barriers, but in a manner very different from globalizing capitalism.[1]

Previous chapters discussed the moral and spiritual imperative for Christians to be engaged with poverty reduction. This chapter focuses on the very real possibility — as judged by those outside the church —

---

1. Vinoth Ramachandra, "Globalization: Towards a Theological Perspective and Critique," Micah Network document published at *www.micahnetwork.org*.

that Christians' increased engagement could leave a lasting imprint on global poverty and indeed on the planet, as Ricardo Navarro's opening story graphically illustrates.

The broken body

We can begin to visualize the body of Christ as his broken body hanging on the cross. Christ's brokenness symbolizes our brokenness as a church, as a human community, as a planet. The body of Christ is not the healthy, cohesive, and unified entity that Paul might have envisaged. Looking at one part of the body — the church — it is fractured into many denominations and traditions, and further bitter divisions form within these. In fact, thirty-four thousand separate Christian groups have been identified in the world.[2] This damaged body needs healing, and part of the healing is to rediscover how to work together in building God's kingdom on earth.

The media, which thrive on conflict and scandal, often report on the inward-looking, small-minded, and hypocritical aspects of Christian communal life. Many who are attracted to Christianity for the best of motives are disappointed when they visit the local churches. As Bryant Myers puts it, "Our greatest pain comes when we wish our work to be part of the sign of the kingdom, expressed through the local church, and yet find ourselves with a church that is unwilling or unable to be this sign with us."[3] When churches wonder why spiritual seekers look outside organized religion, part of the answer is that the churches are not adequately feeding their spiritual hunger.

On the other hand, there is something compelling and inspiring about a gathering of people of faith — especially when it brings together young and old, men and women, and people of different classes, family situations, races, intellects, personalities, sexual orientations, and physical strengths. Faith communities offer a sense of possibility because of the values they teach and to which they aspire — gentleness, kindness, purity, generosity, and hope.

This feeling of ambiguity toward the church is shared by many socially committed Christians, and that knowledge in itself can be somehow comforting. David Bosch, who calls the church "an inseparable union of the divine and the dusty," describes the contradictory feelings that people

---

2. David Barrett, George T. Kurian, and Todd M. Johnson, *World Christian Encyclopedia: A Comparative Survey of Churches and Religions in the Modern World*, 2nd ed. (Oxford and New York: Oxford University Press, 2001).

3. Bryant L. Myers, *Walking with the Poor: Principles and Practices of Transformational Development* (Maryknoll, N.Y.: Orbis Books, 1999), 39.

have about the church: "We can be utterly disgusted, at times," he says, "with the earthliness of the church, yet we can also be transformed, at times, with the awareness of the divine in the church."[4]

?? QUESTION FOR DISCUSSION

♦ What do you understand by the body of Christ? Who are members of it? How do you feel about its divisions?

Our hunger is for the church to be more of a living sacrament in the world and more of a beacon of social and moral values for our fellow human beings and for the world in which we live. As we must care for our fellow human beings, so too must we care for our planet and acknowledge our interdependence with the rest of the created order. This outlook resonates with the Millennium Development Goals, which also acknowledge that the well-being of humanity is closely related to the way we interact with the rest of creation. And so the seventh goal addresses several aspects of caring for the environment that impinge directly on the lives of the poor.

MDGs

Goal 7: Ensure environmental sustainability

This goal has three quite different subtargets:

Target 1: Integrate the principles of sustainable development into country policies and programs and reverse the loss of environmental resources.

Target 2: Halve by 2015 the proportion of people without sustainable access to safe drinking water and basic sanitation (1.1 billion people do not drink safe water, and 2.6 billion lack sanitation).

Target 3: By 2020, to have achieved a significant improvement in the lives of at least 100 million slum dwellers.

These targets are very different. The first target responds to the growing evidence that human activity is degrading and destabilizing the natural environment. For example, a scientific consensus is emerging that the output of carbon dioxide (CO_2) from factories, power stations, vehicles, etc., is causing

---

4. David Bosch, cited in ibid., 39.

global warming, and with it, significant changes in weather patterns and sea levels. Another problem is the rate of depletion of forests, which not only compounds global warming because trees absorb carbon dioxide but is also associated with the increased risk of the "natural disasters" of flooding and landslides.

The second target acknowledges that at present 40 percent of the world's people do not have access to sanitation, by far the most of these in Asia. About 20 percent of countries are on track, but progress will need to accelerate in order to meet the goal. Again, only Latin America and the Caribbean among all the regions appears to be on track.

The third target is to improve the lives of 100 million slum dwellers through better sanitation and secure land tenure systems. About 924 million people live in slums across the world — an increase of 200 million from 1990.

Slum dwellers in millions

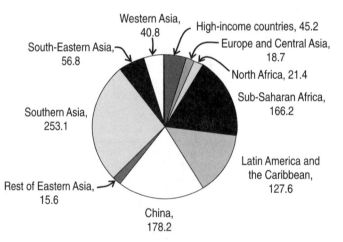

Source: UN Statistics Division, "World and Regional Trends," Millennium Indicators Database, *http://millenniumindicators.un.org* (accessed May 2005); based on data provided by UN-HABITAT.

How are we doing so far? Progress varies considerably.

In aggregate terms, the targets for clean water and sanitation lie within reach, with East Asia, South Asia, and Latin America on track, although Sub-Saharan Africa lags. However, the data on the other targets are weak, and progress is slow.

A view from the outside

As the church wants to serve the world, so the world wants to work with the church in building up our common life. While many in the West are skeptical of organized religion, development agencies that are interested in effectively reducing poverty have become increasingly interested in the role religious groups play in international development. So it is that the World Bank, the US Agency for International Development, the UK Department for International Development, the World Health Organization, the International Labor Organization, the Inter-American Development Bank and many other international organizations now seek to collaborate with religious leaders and their communities. The reasons for their interest are simple. Even though participation in religion may be in decline in parts of the West, it is growing rapidly in many parts of the world, building a powerful network of hope, information, and action for change.

Why is this happening now? Part of the answer lies in what faith communities can offer practically in poor contexts in developing countries. Viewed from the outside, churches and other faith-based groups can be effective partners in poverty reduction. As Jim Wolfensohn, then president of the World Bank, said to a gathering of bishops, "Together we can do a lot. We have expertise. You [religious leaders and faith communities] have expertise. We know a lot about development.... You have the best distribution system of any NGO in the world. You are out there in the fields with your flocks, you and other religions."[5]

Wolfensohn is correct. Faith-based groups are present across the world, and by being in the heart of communities they are often in direct relationship with the poorest of the poor. For a development agency it can actually be quite difficult to reach the "extreme" poor because they tend to be very busy, or very young or old, or constrained in other ways. But faith leaders know the poor as members of their communities. They live alongside them; they see them at worship and in their homes; they visit and try to assist those who are ill, those who are abused within the family, orphans, and widows, and those who cannot afford the basics of life. They are present with their people.

Faith-based communities are also active in providing practical care for the poor. The first volume of the *Voices of the Poor* study of how poor people describe their poverty experience found that they often obtain material support from religious institutions:

5. *The Official Report of the Lambeth Conference, 1998* (Harrisburg, Pa.: Morehouse, 1999), 352.

In some regions, NGOs with the strongest presence are religiously affiliated. This is the case for instance in Benin, where these organizations function as one of the most visible and widely distributed institutional safety nets for the poor. "The majority of the orphanages are run by Catholic sisters, the only country-wide nutritional program is managed by Cathwell, and several programs to assist the sick, the abandoned, and the destitute have been set up by nuns and priests. In Cotonou, the Catholic Church is arguably the strongest presence helping the most vulnerable." In Panama, over half the communities recognized churches and schools for their support. In Vietnam, poor Catholic households in need of support turned to the church. In Pakistan, the [Participatory Poverty Assessment] reports "a deeply entrenched tradition of private charity and welfare reinforced by Islamic religious obligation." Mosques and shrines were valued as sites of charity. Ashrams were mentioned in some places in India as places of refuge for the poor.[6]

Furthermore, faith-based groups attract volunteers and may therefore be more cost-effective than secular organizations. Religious workers can also be — at least in some cases — highly motivated to serve by powerful guiding principles. For example, "The Pentecostal Church [in Bulgaria] is reputed to be the 'Gypsy Church' and is singled out as helping poor people and those who were ill; its pastors go out into the community to be with poor people despite the fact that they have their own children to feed."[7] To give another example of how religious beliefs can make a difference, a study on health care in Uganda by the Center for Economic Policy and Research in Washington, D.C., found that despite being paid lower wages, staff of religious not-for-profit organizations were more likely to charge less than other providers and to use the resulting additional funding to decrease fees and increase services, not raise their own salaries.[8] Here we can see how an ethic of solidarity can affect professional as well as voluntary work.

Of course, some faith-based communities are also patriarchal, prejudiced, or inefficient, and no more immune than other human groups from financial and personal scandal. Yet empirically, across countries

---

6. Deepa Narayan et al., *Voices of the Poor: Can Anyone Hear Us?* (New York: Oxford University Press for the World Bank, 2000), 105; see also Deepa Narayan, Robert Chambers, Meera K. Shah, and Patti Petesch, *Voices of the Poor: Crying Out for Change* (New York: Oxford University Press for the World Bank, 2000).

7. Narayan et al., *Voices of the Poor: Crying Out for Change*, 223.

8. Ritva Reinikka and Jakob Svensson, *Working for God? Evaluating Service Delivery of Religious Not-for-Profit Health Care Providers in Uganda*, Center for Economic Policy and Research Discussion Paper 4214 (Washington, D.C.: World Bank, 2003).

and denominations, faith communities have an immediate relevance to the poor. In a study across twenty countries of the institutions that poor people found to be "important" and "effective" in their lives, religious organizations ranked as the second best out of fourteen categories (the best were community organizations in which poor people participated, such as women's and men's organizations, or athletic organizations). In this study the poor considered religious organizations to be more important and effective than their kin and family, local leaders, NGOs, shops and moneylenders, private enterprise and traders, banks, politicians, police, health services, schools, or various government agencies.

Across countries, the strengths of religious organizations were deemed to be their responsiveness to the poor, their trustworthiness, their respect for the poor, their honesty and fairness, and their attitudes of caring, loving, and listening. They ranked poorly in the extent to which they empowered poor people to participate in decision making and to help themselves. They were also deemed to be less accountable to local communities, and often they did not foster unity but rather created conflict.[9] So the record of faith-based communities is mixed, but on the whole very positive — and with great potential.

Some have called the church "the first NGO," and indeed in many ways it is. As we have seen throughout this book, and particularly in this chapter, religious groups can respond to poverty with great spiritual and social resources. What's more, the transnational nature of faith communities and institutions makes them particularly suitable for dealing with poverty reduction.

Understanding this potential is important for several reasons. First of all, many churches in the UK and US have already developed long-term relationships with faith communities overseas. Because they recognize that religious institutions are good at reaching and building relationships with the poor, secular agencies are seeking to support faith groups in development work. Thus churches may wish to explore existing overseas relationships with poverty reduction in mind, or form new partnerships with churches that are deeply engaged in reducing extreme poverty. There are plenty of examples at the end of this chapter, and throughout this book, to stimulate the building of new connections.

Second, when we turn to advocacy and larger-scale social action for the MDGs, again, it may be important — as well as natural — for churches across countries to communicate and collaborate with one another.

---

9. Narayan et al., *Voices of the Poor: Crying Out for Change*, 184.

Whatever Happened to Liberation Theology?

You heard about it vaguely — maybe it wasn't your style or maybe it was. But what happened to liberation theology? Well, in a nutshell:

◆ It went into a crisis with the collapse of socialism.

◆ It separated theology from economic ideology.

◆ It retained its commitment to the poor.

◆ It has reemerged on every continent — sometimes called "contextual theology."

◆ It focuses on civil society and advocacy — the subjects of this chapter.

Here a few of the leaders of liberation theology tell about their journey:

"What has happened to the 'irruption of the poor' so enthusiastically announced in the 1970s by Latin American liberationists? Whence cometh the revolution of the impoverished and oppressed majorities so eagerly awaited and vociferously proclaimed?"[a]

...it went into crisis initially

"Latin American liberationist thought is in crisis; it has run up against the end of history, the triumph of savage capitalism....Latin American liberationists do not deny this unpleasant reality....Leonardo Boff writes about 'the general crisis in left-wing thought' brought on by the collapse of socialism and Jon Sobrino observes that we are witnessing the closing of a period that was shot through with the hope and praxis of historical liberation. Pablo Richard recognizes a complete collapse of hope that renders the current situation 'worse than it was at the outset of the conquest.' Franz Hinkelammert speaks of 'capitalism without alternatives' and Javier Iguíñez laments the fading of the irruption of the poor and the weakening of the liberating process."[b]

But then:

...it separated economics and theology pragmatically, and dropped its ideological stance

"Theologically, there is nothing sacrosanct about *any* economic (or theological) system.... Suffice it to say, the demands for economic justice

---

a. Daniel M. Bell, *Liberation Theology after the End of History: The Refusal to Cease Suffering* (London and New York: Routledge, 2001), 43.
b. Ibid.

have shifted from the ideological debates of the 1970s and 1980s to a more pragmatic struggle with economic realities — to which there appear to be no simple or quick solutions. For liberation theology to meet this challenge it must build on the pragmatism, social critique and the democratic impulses that have permeated this theological debate from its inception, rather than its ideological, doctrinaire dimensions."[c]

...it kept the commitment to the poor

"Poverty is still a central problem for the global economy in the post cold war world.... So in the economic sphere, at least, ... this theology is not a passing fashion. Its corollary — oppression — is unfortunately not a fashion but rather a growing problem. The theology of liberation is thus still very necessary, because Christian faith must today respond with credibility — and theological rationality — to the oldest and newest question as posed by Gutiérrez: how to tell the poor that God loves them."[d]

...it reemerged on every continent, sometimes called contextual theology

"The themes of economic justice and the spiritual empowerment of the poor continue to be relevant to the period of reconstruction in South Africa, eastern Europe, Latin America, and elsewhere. These situations require, however, that these themes be developed in relation to the contextual changes that have taken place."[e]

"Contextual theology is a term now widely used to designate theological reflection which explicitly explores the dialogue between social context and Scripture and tradition."[f]

...it focuses on civil society and advocacy

In the words of Pablo Richard: "A new space for solidarity is *civil society*. In this space it is not a matter of seizing power, but rather of constructing a new power, from the social movements, with a logic distinct from that of the market. From civil society we can fight to reconstruct the state, a democratic state at the service of the common good, at the service of the life of all, especially the excluded and nature."[g]

---

c. Charles Villa-Vicencio, in Christopher Rowland, ed., *The Cambridge Companion to Liberation Theology* (Cambridge: Cambridge University Press, 1999), 163.

d. Ignacio Ellacuría and Jon Sobrino, quoted in Rowland, ed., *The Cambridge Companion to Liberation Theology*, 232.

e. Charles Villa-Vicencio in Rowland, ed., *The Cambridge Companion to Liberation Theology*, 163.

f. Rowland, ed., *The Cambridge Companion to Liberation Theology*, xiii–xiv.

g. Cited in Bell, *Liberation Theology after the End of History*, 69.

Third, although this book does not address domestic poverty in the US or the UK, it may be that the experiences of engaged churches in the global South could strengthen and enrich UK and US churches' work to address their own poverty.

"Together we can do a lot"

So far we have focused primarily on the churches in the developing countries. But what about churches in the West? In previous chapters we discussed the moral and spiritual imperative for Christians to engage with poverty reduction. This chapter observes the very real possibility — as judged by those outside the church — that the church's increased engagement will leave a lasting imprint on global poverty. This message needs to be heard — and acted upon. As Bishop Arthur Walmsley, a leader in Episcopalians for Global Reconciliation, said:

> There have been . . . moments . . . in our lifetime when a popular uprising based on a passion for justice or a drive against violence has turned the corner in the world's life, which not only defied entrenched systems of domination but astonished and transformed our own apprehension that truth and goodness cannot prevail.[10]

Two very different examples offer considerable optimism about the role churches and other faith communities can play in working toward the MDGs. Together, they demonstrate how churches can approach the issue of poverty reduction effectively, but in very different ways. The first example is a voluntary religious organization that has established an excellent reputation and is often considered as a case study for the role of religious groups in international development and conflict resolution. This is the Italian community of Sant'Egidio, a Rome-based lay Catholic religious community with an international humanitarian focus. Founded in 1968, the community prays every night for peace and an end to suffering in the world, and it keeps the gospel and the poor at the core of its prayers. From its humble beginnings as a group of high school students, the community is now forty thousand strong, and communities have sprung up across Africa, Asia, and the Americas.

While the Community of Sant'Egidio began as a charity organization in Italy, giving food and shelter to the urban poor on the outskirts of Rome, in the 1980s it extended its reach by raising donations and

---

10. Arthur Walmsley, "Opening Remarks on Episcopalians for Global Reconciliation," Trinity Church, Boston, March 23, 2004.

offering aid to the impoverished peoples of southern Africa, particularly Mozambique. By the 1990s the community had developed such a strong relationship with the two warring parties in Mozambique that the community was able to broker a peace settlement to end that country's seventeen-year-old civil war and so to continue to deliver the necessary humanitarian aid. Because of its success in Mozambique, the community has since brokered peace agreements in such countries as Algeria, Rwanda, and Guatemala. In recognition of its work, the community has on a number of occasions been nominated for the Nobel Peace Prize. Yet if you ask members of the community, they will tell you that prayer and following the gospel are the two most important tenets of the life of the community, and all else proceeds from that point. Out of the forty thousand members of the community around the world, whether they are negotiating a settlement, working in the community's Rome soup kitchen, or working with the elderly, only a handful receive any remuneration for their time.[11]

The second, and very different, example of a successful church initiative is the recent campaign for economic justice known as Jubilee 2000 or Drop the Debt. Jubilee 2000 began because Christians were concerned with the crippling effects of unsustainable debts owed by developing nations to lending institutions and governments. For various reasons, including money peddling on one side and corruption on the other, these debts had become so unmanageable that the interest repayments themselves accounted for a large proportion of the country's public expenditure, diverting funds away from health, education, and other essential services. The objective of Jubilee 2000 was to ask for these debts to be canceled. This objective was inspired by the principle of debt remission, or Jubilee, found in Leviticus and Deuteronomy, which was designed to bring relief to the poor by a radical form of redistribution every fifty years.

Starting with a handful of people, and subsequently powerfully endorsed by Pope John Paul II and the Catholic Church (among many others), Jubilee 2000 reached its tipping point in 1996. Jubilee 2000 captured the zeitgeist and spread through the electronic media to involve 24 million people worldwide in signing a petition for debt remission. Across the world Christian organizations championed the cause. One memorable moment in the campaign was "Hands Around Birmingham," when tens of thousands of people joined hands and encircled the city cen-

---

11. From the Web site of the Community of Sant'Egidio, *www.santegidio.org/en.*

ter of Birmingham, UK, in 1998. Inside the circle of hands, hearts, minds, and souls the leaders of the most powerful countries of the world — the "Group of 8" or G-8 — were expected to make important decisions about debt relief. Hands Around Birmingham was a powerful symbolic action that sent out a clear message to world leaders: tread carefully, and consider the poor.

Jubilee 2000 achieved a degree of success. Projected debt relief will total $55 billion. To date $29 billion has been provided, though low-income countries still hold $523 billion in debt. Jubilee 2000's legacy has been to raise public awareness of international economics and poverty issues, to make a good-faith effort to channel debt relief into poverty reduction, and to prevent it from diversion to private or military interests. From humble beginnings, Jubilee 2000 caught on and captured attention. From Bono to Bill Clinton, from Pope John Paul II to the casual newspaper reader, Jubilee 2000 and Drop the Debt defined an important moment in the lives of millions and will certainly be viewed alongside civil rights, anti-slavery, anti-apartheid, and other moral campaigns providing inspiration for others to tackle seemingly intractable social ills.

Just as quickly as it emerged, however, so the Jubilee movement has disappeared from the public eye, even though debt remains a serious problem. A sequel to Jubilee 2000 is still at work but has a low profile. By failing to follow through or inform people of the outcome of the debt campaign, the movement failed to capitalize on the goodwill and momentum it had mobilized. Nevertheless, it has left an important legacy, and hopefully the energy and interest it generated can be rekindled to help achieve the MDGs.

While Jubilee 2000 had a clear purpose, the turn of the millennium was also a period of unprecedented international activism on wider issues surrounding globalization. From the World Trade Organization (WTO) meeting in Seattle in 1999 until September 11, 2001, every major meeting of the WTO or the World Bank or G-8 became a site of major protests. What was the focus of these protests? It is not quite clear. There were many voices, including church groups and anarchists, yet there seemed to be an inchoate, somewhat inarticulate sense that the current distribution of economic resources was unjust and needed to be deeply challenged. The benefits of globalization were accruing to the "haves," and the "have-nots" were being passed over (and in the process the environment was being stripped). The economist Amartya Sen tried to clarify what he understood the underlying issue to be. The real problem, he concluded, was not globalization but "inequity . . . which produces very unequal sharing of the benefits of globalization. The question is not just whether the poor, too, gain something from globalization, but whether they gain a fair share."[12] The conclusion—of Sen as well as of the anti-globalization protesters—was that the poor are not gaining a fair share and that vigorous public protest could change it.

Partly due to the momentum that Jubilee 2000 created, the need for urgent attention to issues of economic justice was acknowledged by the Anglican Church at an international gathering of all its bishops in 1998. At that year's Lambeth Conference Jim Wolfensohn addressed the meeting and answered hard questions related to the World Bank's role in debt relief for the poorest nations. The longest, most detailed resolution of that meeting "called for a comprehensive response from the bishops to address international debt including engagement with political and corporate leaders on the issue and the funding of international development programs at a level of at least 0.7 percent of annual total diocesan income."[13] The Lambeth Conference had been dominated by a divisive dispute over the church's attitude to homosexuality. Against this background, the resolution on "International Debt and Economic Justice" provided a welcome opportunity for solidarity. The archbishop of Cape Town, Njongonkulu Ndungane, summed up the situation well when he said:

> Observe, my brothers and sisters, that the world is waiting for a word of hope, of encouragement. The world longs to hear good news for the poor and recovery of sight to the blind, and to know that now is the year of the Lord's favour. What will the bishops give them? Bitter, distressing words of conflict...? The world already has more of that than it can bear.
>
> What the bishops can give them is one voice, a voice strong in defense of the poor, bold in contradiction to the rule of money, and full of the love of God.[14]

In the UK, the Lambeth Conference added considerable weight to the Jubilee 2000 campaign. In the US, the Episcopal Church, together with other Anglican leaders, contributed to the "drafting and passage

---

12. Amartya Sen, from Lecture 2 of the Ishizaka Lectures given on February 2, 2002, in Tokyo. This lecture was entitled "Global Inequality and Human Security."

13. *The Official Report of the Lambeth Conference, 1998* (Harrisburg, Pa.: Morehouse, 1999), 384–87.

14. Ibid., 359.

of the most comprehensive international debt-relief legislation ever presented to the United States Congress."[15] Not only that, but it helped sow the seeds for a new movement that is now emerging in the Episcopal Church.

?? QUESTION FOR DISCUSSION

◆ How do you think that the task of reducing poverty can be a unifying influence among and within churches?

Episcopalians for Global Reconciliation

At the turn of the new millennium a group of Episcopalians in the US came together to explore how the church could pursue global reconciliation through economic justice. By chance, this group met directly after September 11, 2001, and the dreadful events of that day sharpened the group's focus. Out of this meeting, Episcopalians for Global Reconciliation (EGR) was formed. In the first description of "why we are meeting" they wrote, "America — the country we love — stands at the center of this problem. There is little sense of the need for a massive reallocation of our national resources, and much resistance to a major reshaping of our political and economic priorities in light of the deteriorating world situation."[16] The group that emerged was described by Jeffrey Rowthorn, former bishop of the Convocation of American Churches in Europe, as a "Church-based, intergenerational network of economists, business people, bishops and parish clergy, social organizers, theologians and people working with the United Nations and other agencies concerned with global economic development. Individually and corporately, we each sense an urgent need for a significant shift in the economic and social priorities of our Church, and our nation."[17]

EGR aims to teach young and old, conservative and liberal, seeker and doubter, cradle Episcopalian and convert about global poverty and then empower them with concrete possibilities for action. It also advocates 0.7 percent giving at the personal, church, and national level. EGR's deeper intention is spiritual renewal, as it believes that spiritual renewal

---

15. Ian Douglas in Ian Douglas, Richard Parker, Jeffrey Rowthorn, and Arthur Walmsley, "Why We Are Meeting," unpublished paper, 2002, p. 14.

16. Ibid.

17. Unpublished paper, Episcopalians for Global Reconciliation.

and action on behalf of those in extreme poverty are inherently linked. It seeks to reawaken the Episcopal Church's role as a moral leader, to mobilize the political will necessary to pursue policies that advance economic justice. As Arthur Walmsley commented, "Changing government policies will not come easily. Changing our own is a matter of will, and of faith."[18]

Episcopalians for Global Reconciliation quickly aligned itself to the Millennium Development Goals, recognizing that they contained an appropriate vision for the church as well as a practical and feasible plan of how groups in the rich societies could contribute to their realization. Furthermore, the MDGs represent a vision that can be embraced by Christians who hold a range of theological and political views. Remarkably, EGR intentionally brings together church leaders and members who hold conflicting views on sexuality but who find agreement and common purpose about the Christian obligation to the poor. To return to the image of the body of Christ, EGR's composition and focus on the MDGs is most of all a recognition of the power of concerted collective action and of the interconnectedness of God's children in spite of our diversity. The church's initiative has been welcomed by the United Nations and other secular as well as church-based groups, and is the very antithesis of what the late Valerie Pitt called "the fatal Anglican habit of directing the energies of the devout into self-cultivation and controversy."[19] With the Millennium Development Goals, the church has a clear mission focus in the world.

There are several notable features about EGR. Most important is that its starting point is spiritual renewal. EGR is in harmony with the ethos of this book in that it regards poverty reduction as fundamental to Christian discipleship and as a means of engaging with God at a profound level. In this respect, EGR is not only enriching the church spiritually, but providing a focus of unity in these times of tension and division. Also significant is that EGR seeks to influence the church at all levels. Like Jubilee 2000, it is a grassroots movement. But unlike Jubilee 2000, it is permeating church structures and aims to be a long-term social movement. It calls on all parts of the church to engage with the MDGs, from local action and involvement to its leaders' taking a prominent national role in speaking up for the poor. In these respects, EGR offers a model for how other churches could — and should — engage with poverty reduction.

---

18. Unpublished paper, Episcopalians for Global Reconciliation.
19. Cited in J. Rowthorn, "Tract for Our Times," EGR Web page, *www.e4gr.org.*

The Micah Challenge

Another church-based, MDG-focused organization, the Micah Challenge, works across denominations. Inspired by Micah 6:8, "What does the Lord require of you but to do justice, and to love kindness, and to walk humbly with your God," the Micah Challenge is a global campaign focusing on the MDGs and is facilitated by the World Evangelical Alliance and the Micah Network (a consortium of over 250 evangelical Christian organizations providing relief, development, and justice ministries throughout the world). Launched in October 2004, Micah is an emerging network supporting national campaigns to reduce poverty, linking up to 160 million evangelical Christians across the world. The network sees in the MDGs an example of God's "integral mission," described in chapter 4, which includes a call to God's people to advocate and act to reduce poverty and suffering. The network has enormous potential, given the tremendous motivation and commitment of evangelical Christians.

The Global Call for Action to Address Poverty

EGR, Jubilee groups, and the Micah Challenge are among many organizations contributing to the Global Call to Action to Address Poverty campaigns that are taking place across the world. In the UK, a broad coalition of over fifty groups has galvanized this into Make Poverty History, with a strong focus on 2005, the year in which Britain hosts the G-8 Summit, holds the presidency of the European Union, and the Africa Commission — initiated by Tony Blair — released its report. Make Poverty History focuses on trade, debt, and aid, the major components of Goal 8 of the MDGs. Campaign leaders include at least thirteen Christian agencies: the Mothers' Union, Christian Aid, CAFOD, Tearfund, Trócaire, World Vision, Scottish Catholic International Aid Fund, Methodist Relief and Development Fund, Leprosy Mission, United Reformed Church, Unitarian and Free Christian Church, Church of Scotland Board of World Mission, and the Viva Network.

The UK campaign, like Jubilee 2000, involves many others than people of faith, yet the churches' presence is disproportionately high within the coalition. Unlike Jubilee 2000, Make Poverty History has had a high media profile and explicit government support. Its goals are also larger and the campaign stronger, and with the increase in media advocacy and networking, lasting change is wholly plausible. One way that the campaign has gained public attention was to feature in the New Year special of the popular television comedy *The Vicar of Dibley*. Crossing the boundaries of fact and fiction, the actress Dawn French, who stars as the Reverend Geraldine Granger in the comedy, led a delegation of four hundred real-life women priests from the Church of England to deliver a petition on poverty to the prime minister in January 2005. As might be imagined, this delegation captured the headlines and the public imagination, as did its events surrounding the G-8 Summit in Scotland in July 2005.

In the United States, the campaign has taken on the title the ONE Campaign and has embarked on a massive advocacy effort to rally Americans behind the goal of ending extreme poverty. "ONE is a new effort by Americans," its mission statement reads, "to rally Americans — one by one — to fight the emergency of global AIDS and extreme poverty." Launched by U2's Bono, the ONE Campaign gathers faith leaders, musicians, actors, and politicians to work for the end of extreme poverty and the achievement of the Millennium Development Goals.

The message of these and other national campaigns is a powerful one. In the middle of the minute-long television piece that the ONE Campaign ran on the major American television networks in the spring of 2005, the presiding bishop of the Episcopal Church, the Most Rev. Frank Griswold, spoke "one" single word: "together." To take the word "together" with the word "one" is to be at the defining center of this book. We live on one planet, we are bound as one in the body of Christ, and it is up to each one of us to envision a world where poverty is history. One person acts in mission with God and with all other concerned peoples, Christian or otherwise. Together, as one, we can accomplish a lot.

Concluding Thoughts

This chapter has shown that many churches are already deeply involved in poverty reduction. Yet the thrust of this book is that much more can be done if more people join in and if poverty reduction becomes part of the warp and weft of everyday Christian discipleship, as we have argued it should be. There is much we can do together: initiatives such as EGR and the Micah Challenge offer two clear models for how this can be achieved, within and across churches of very different styles and traditions.

This chapter has also shown how secular agencies are keen to work in partnership with churches and faith-based groups on matters of common concern, both in developed and developing countries. This is significant, as it greatly increases the potential for achieving results. It is also an extremely valuable opportunity for Christian witness, for it enables secular partners to gain an insight into church life and Christian discipleship. It is therefore important that in working with such partners we are faithful witnesses to the gospel.

The next action also offers a practical way of witnessing to Christian faith, and, like those women priests mentioned earlier, to make a statement of concern and commitment to the poor. It is time to stand up and be counted!

?? **QUESTION FOR DISCUSSION**

◆ Have you joined a church-based campaign? If not, why not? If you have, what was the experience like?

ACTION 6:
STAND UP AND BE COUNTED

The media have a direct impact on public imagination. Statements by politicians, religious leaders, and artists consistently shape our interpretation of reality. In this media-framed world, a message delivered by symbolic action can leave an imprint on the mind and change the course of events. Newspapers, magazines, television — even church newsletters — documented the history of social change in the twentieth century. Think of the nonviolent march to Selma during the civil rights movement in the United States. Think of the lone Chinese youth who stood still before an army of tanks in Tiananmen Square or the "Orange Revolution" in the Ukraine, which peacefully ushered in a new era of democratic leadership in a country unfamiliar with freedom. We know of these events largely through the media. Not only did each event convey a powerful "No" to oppression and the abuse of human rights, all sent a clear moral message to the world, and that message was carried by the media.

Poverty deserves its own broadcast. This action asks you to take part in a peaceful, strategic, popular, and widespread event designed to express effective support for poverty reduction. Besides helping you create your own action, we will also tell you about the meaning of the white armband, which can be worn on particular dates, to show your commitment to fighting poverty. There are many rich opportunities for creative organizing and for making a difference in the public mind.

Mass gatherings can seem alarmist and the preserve of a fringe group of activists. It is not of these that we speak. Many collective symbolic actions involve a wide range of people, as was the case in Selma and the Ukraine, and often include church members. Even the body of Christ meets for symbolic collective action — to break bread together, to hold an outdoor service, or sometimes to process in the streets.

Why is this strategic? It builds political will.

There are a limited number of reasons for which people come together in massive groups on a public issue. One is to create political will. Global poverty would not be expensive to reduce. Nor are the barriers to poverty reduction technical; we know what to do. The reason for slow progress is a lack of political will. In balancing competing demands from different people and groups, businesses, governments, and other powerful actors do not devote sufficient attention and resources to the problem of poverty. Direct action can create a moral counterweight to indifference and appeal not only to the altruism of leaders but also to their self-interest. Politicians need to be reelected. Corporations need to retain clients and to appear socially responsible. Leaders must be held accountable to the public. Collective action can therefore generate momentum among them.

What does direct action achieve?

By acting together about a shared concern, people can *make* an issue seem important and make it visible so that it attracts media attention and others can be informed and inspired to learn. When direct actions include people from diverse backgrounds (age, economic status, profession, gender), they communicate a powerful sense of unanimity. People acting together on the basis of a moral insight can raise political will. They have in the past, and they can again.

Is this still true? The antiwar protests in 2003 that drew over a hundred thousand protesters worldwide did not immediately shift the course of events. Protests are rarely immediately decisive. Yet this event is remembered again and again by political leaders (especially as they come up for election). Furthermore, and significantly, the protests were covered in the Arab media — and affected public opinion. For example, the presence of Christian leaders in the protests worked to counteract the widespread perception in the Arab world that the war was a religious war against Islam. So whatever your position was on the Iraq war, one lesson that cannot be drawn is that the collective presence of more than one hundred thousand persons availed nothing. Direct action retains a significant, although not an absolute, power.

Central to this power is the fact that big events can be seen on TV screens worldwide. When the impoverished see their hardship objected to by far-off strangers it may change their perception of people in the West. It may also engender hope. Knowing that you are not alone in a struggle is transformative. As we have said throughout this book, to be effective one person must take the trouble to act in tandem with others. Nowhere is this more obvious than in direct action.

The obligation to act stems also from the recognition that a truth must be shared, even if it fails. As the prophet Jeremiah put it, "Within me there is something like a burning fire shut up in my bones. I am weary with holding it in; indeed, I cannot" (Jeremiah 20:9). The reactions of fellow Israelites were not a factor to Jeremiah. He had to speak, even if he was ignored. When Mahatma Gandhi was a young lawyer protesting about voting restrictions in South Africa, he said, "Even if you are in a minority of one, the truth is still the truth." It must be voiced.

Truth is perhaps the most powerful element in collective action. The civil rights movement in the United States named evil and spoke powerfully against it, using marches, sit-ins, boycotts, and other forms of nonviolent direct action. The global anti-apartheid movement brought moral, political, and economic pressure to bear on South Africa, and that pressure eventually weakened and led to the demise of that cruel system. Women's suffrage movements were effective in hastening the extension of the vote to women in many countries. Throughout history we can find examples of successful collective action against the odds. They are full of inspiration. The truth has a power of its own. We can help it to prevail.

Wear a white band

The symbol for the Global Call to Action Against Poverty, the ONE Campaign, and Make Poverty History is a white band — armband, headband, wrist band, or any other form of band. People are asked to wear the white band on certain specified dates (September 10, December 10 in 2005) as a universal symbol of commitment to meeting the MDGs and making poverty history. Wear it to work; wear it on the playground; wear it to the pub; wear it to do your shopping. Wherever you go, be ready to explain — briefly and succinctly — what it's for. If enough people wear the white armband (and millions are already doing so) it will raise awareness and increase the political will to fight poverty. If the public understands an issue and wants to bring about change, then politicians and decision-makers will feel the heat and the pressure to act. Many of us may not be the "type" to decorate ourselves with buttons and ribbons. It is all the more powerful a symbol if we humble ourselves to do so on this occasion.

From large-scale demonstrations and marches to more intimate vigils to a white armband to a small red ribbon, a decision to participate directly expresses your solidarity and care. By lending your voice and your presence to the cause you cannot be counted as silent nor presumed to be a tacit supporter of the inequitable status quo. By your symbolic action, you light a candle, either literally or figuratively, against the darkness of indifference.

Web sites

International: *www.whiteband.org*

UK: *www.makepovertyhistory.org/*

US: *www.onecampaign.org*

7

On Giants' Shoulders:
Stories to Inspire

Lost in Translation: A Cautionary Tale of Reconstruction and Reconciliation in a Muslim Country

"God sees your good work and He is pleased," Khari Barakatullah Salim, a full-bearded Afghan imam in robes and wraparound sunglasses, assures us.

We're sitting on rugs rolled out across the shady corner of the Public Mosque of Quarabagh's unfinished concrete porch. The July 2003 day is still, parched, as we look across this mountain-ringed plain north of Kabul. Our group includes myself (an Episcopal clergywoman from Manhattan), four other Americans — three of whom are sweating under clumsily wrapped head scarves — four or five mosque elders, and our Afghan American translator. Twenty-five white-robed *talib* (literally, students of the Qur'an) sit in a semicircle around Khari Barakatullah, the blind Mullah whose Qur'anic recitations open Afghanistan's daily national television broadcasts. Piled before us on large plates are welcoming slices of yellow and pink melon, the fruit so delicious that American agribusiness tried to duplicate it in California.

Khari Barakatullah's words flood me with confidence. The "good work" he refers to is the almost-completed mosque where we are picnicking on the porch. Following the September 11, 2001, attacks on the World Trade Center and Pentagon, the Episcopal Diocese of New York's two-year interfaith effort to rebuild an Afghan mosque destroyed by US bombs is indeed a brave, if difficult beginning of a cross-cultural conversation between Christians and Muslims. The complexities of negotiating with temperamental contractors from fifteen thousand miles away fade for a moment. Likewise, the nagging doubts I brought along lighten up. (Why were we rebuilding a mosque in Afghanistan when church roofs still leaked in New York?) Even the ongoing struggle to dispel Afghan misperceptions about Christians' motives loses some of its urgency. The morning is still and hot. We eat our melon and begin to talk.

Communion had not always been so sweet.

As happens, our honeymoon with Mr. Fayaz, the contractor we engaged to rebuild the mosque, was short-lived. While Mr. Fayaz's low bid and pious enthusiasm had initially impressed our interfaith partners at the Masjid Hazrat-i-Abu Bakr mosque in Flushing, New York, at the ribbon-cutting ceremony, the building was only half finished. We learned thirdhand that Mr. Fayaz had argued with the mosque leadership. Construction stopped even before the minaret (from which the call to prayer is made) was complete. In the summer of 2003 I went to Kabul to try and persuade Mr. Fayaz to finish the job. I went with other Americans and was accompanied by an Afghan American translator, Wahid Omer, who had fled Afghanistan at the age of nineteen.

When I caught sight of the heavyset contractor waiting impatiently for our arrival, I rushed to the door to greet him. After a few moments of sullen silence, Mr. Fayaz rallied and welcomed me to Afghanistan, flinging the corner of his dirty shawl back over one shoulder, placing his callused right hand over his heart, and dipping his head faintly in the graceful way that Afghans acknowledge one another. We walked inside and, sitting cross-legged on cushions, began a difficult conversation.

Producing $7,650 worth of small bills from my travel belt went a long way toward clearing up the basic misunderstandings about work and payment expectations. But what about this problem of communication with the mosque leaders, I asked. My question unleashed a staccato torrent. Construction couldn't continue until the placement of the minaret was decided, but the location of the minaret was in dispute. Fayaz said it belonged in the front of the mosque, but elders disagreed — with him and with one another.

Images of tedious but intransigent vestry arguments over the proper height of pews came to mind. Attempting to be diplomatic, I asked if there was any way for the elders to feel like they were in charge, but for the mullah to make the decision. "Yes," Mr. Fayaz snorted, waving a dismissive hand. He would tell the elders that the "American engineers" had come to town and decreed that the minaret must be in front of the mosque.

I plowed on, trying to shift our talk from positions to interests. What was the real reason the elders wanted the minaret in the back? "Would it really be the end of the world?"

My translator Wahid hesitated and looked at me in a way that suggested he hoped I didn't want him to translate that. When I insisted, he went ahead— and was once again assailed by an animated tirade from the contractor. Finally, Wahid turned to me and said, discreetly, "He has his own way of dealing with things. Afghans only understand power. We will talk about it later."

After we waved Mr. Fayaz on his way, Wahid explained the contractor's solution. In addition to telling the fabricated story about the American engineers, he would pay each elder 120 Afghani. This sum, the equivalent of less than two dollars apiece, would make the problem disappear. The mosque would get its minaret — but hardly as we had imagined.

Some might disagree with the entire idea of Christians rebuilding a mosque. Others might be disappointed by our unorthodox negotiating tactics dictating the minaret's placement. Still others might see the effort as inspirational — for indeed the mosque was rebuilt, by an unprecedented interfaith collaboration. My own evaluation of the project is this: When you go in where angels fear to tread, step lightly, honor your translator, and remember that you are a stranger in a foreign land.

> — *Chloe Breyer. This story is based on the article "Lost in Translation: A Cautionary Tale of Rebuilding in a Muslim Country," originally published in* Slate *magazine, posted February 20, 2004, on www.slate.com.*

Introduction

To Christians, the act of memory is essential for worship. The Anglican priest and social activist Kenneth Leech reminds us that each Sunday, gathered around the altar, we re-member God's broken body on the cross and become, ourselves, the living body of Christ in the world. "Do this in remembrance of me" stands at the heart of Christian liturgy.[1] To be the people God would have us be today, we recall God's role in Creation and God's saving act in history.

Exercising our collective memory is central to our liturgy. Likewise, when we move from the pew to the public square, we must bring with us both the strength of our biblical convictions and a critical understanding of our history. As we act today to change the forces of our world that demean and degrade human dignity, we are called to consider the tactics of successful social reformers and justice seekers of the past — the saints who have gone before us. Do we plan and think as critically as they do? Do we learn from their successes and failures? Do we plumb the past for the lessons they can teach us now?

In this chapter we will explore two Christian social movements from history. The first is the anti-slave-trade campaign associated with William Wilberforce and a group of lay evangelicals called the Clapham Sect at the end of the eighteenth century. The second is the anti-apartheid divestiture campaign and the role of American and South African church leaders in the late 1970s to early 1990s. While separated by time and geography, these church-based social reform movements share common themes. Both movements were international, both involved charismatic leadership from one or more individuals inspired by their faith, and both achieved measurable successes: the end of the legalized slave trade in Great Britain, and the end of apartheid in South Africa. In each movement, however, success came only after several decades of focused work

---

1. Kenneth Leech, *We Preach Christ Crucified* (Cambridge, Mass.: Cowley Publications, 1984), 4.

and initial setbacks. The purpose of this chapter, then, is to bring the achievements and struggles of past church-based social movements to bear on our current work to fight global poverty, recognizing that we are part of a community of faithful people extending through space and time. We are invited to draw wisdom from the saints, living and dead.

William Wilberforce, the Clapham Sect, and the slave trade

William Wilberforce was one of the great political orators of late eighteenth- and early nineteenth-century Britain. His conversion helped change history. As a young member of Parliament from Hull, Wilberforce, aged twenty-six, packed for his holiday reading Dr. Philip Dodderidge's *Rise and Progress of Religion in the Soul*. As a result of his reading he converted to evangelical Christianity. By 1785, while still a parliamentarian (his friend John Newton convinced him not to take holy orders), Wilberforce determined to live a more disciplined Christian life. He withdrew from many of his London social engagements and began to socialize with a group of evangelicals who would later come to be known as the "Clapham Sect."

When Wilberforce started a number of ascetic practices, including two hours of prayer each day and wearing a pebble in his shoe to remind himself of things invisible,[2] friends and family began to worry. Prime Minister William Pitt wrote directly to his friend, "I cannot help expressing my fear that you are nevertheless deluding yourself into principles which . . . render your virtues and yourself both useless to you and mankind."[3]

Wilberforce continued undeterred, however, and a fellow member of the Clapham group, Thomas Clarkson, helped convince him to make the eradication of the slave trade his lifelong quest. Two years after his conversion Wilberforce wrote in his diary, "God, Almighty has set before me two great objects, the suppression of the slave trade and the reformation of manners."[4]

When Wilberforce first proposed a motion in Parliament in 1787 to end the slave trade, British ships transported more than half of the hundred thousand slaves sent each year from Western Africa to the New World.[5] Not only did wealthy businessmen and members of

---

2. G. Lacey May, *Some Eighteenth Century Churchmen* (New York: Macmillan Co., 1920), 216.

3. Jonathan Bayes, "William Wilberforce: His Impact on Nineteenth-Century Society," in *The Churchman* 108, no. 2 (1994): 128.

4. Ibid.

5. Ernest Marshall Howse, *Saints in Politics* (Toronto: University of Toronto Press, 1952), 28.

the aristocracy have a vested financial interest in the slave trade, but the less well-off, including drapers, ropers, grocers, and lawyers, held shares in the smaller slave vessels.[6] Although since 1772 slavery had been ruled illegal in England, the abolition of the slave trade was considered impossibly idealistic.

Steps forward and back along the way

The obstacles to the eradication of the slave trade were daunting. Political leaders were unaware of conditions on the Middle Passage — the journey of slave ships from western Africa across the Atlantic — and were indebted to powerful commercial interests. Despite Wilberforce's tremendous personal enthusiasm, powerful friends, and energy, it was clear a one-man crusade would lead nowhere. He would need the help of his like-minded, public-spirited, evangelical friends.

The Clapham Group or "Sect," as it was later known, was a circle of wealthy evangelical men and women who lived as neighbors in the village of Clapham four miles south of London and who worked together on a number of social reforms. John Venn was the local priest and a spiritual guide to many. Granville Sharp, the leader of the Quaker abolitionists who had successfully led the drive to end slavery in Britain, offered his expertise and firsthand knowledge of the wider reform effort. Thomas Clarkson, confidant and aide to Wilberforce, had written a prize-winning essay on the slave trade while a student at Cambridge University and made abolition his life's work. Hannah More, a religious writer and philanthropist, established vocational schools at a time when popular education programs were unprecedented. These and other individuals supported each other's work and faith and shared time in each other's homes.

Wilberforce turned to these friends — Clarkson in particular — when he realized the extent of Parliament's ignorance about the slave trade's brutality. A member of the House of Lords even claimed that a slave looked upon the Middle Passage as "the happiest period of his life." With the help of William Pitt, Wilberforce set up an official inquiry into the conditions of the slave trade, compiling firsthand accounts and bringing witnesses to give testimony. Once this enormous body of information had been gathered, Clarkson helped Wilberforce prepare for his most powerful and graphic speeches to Parliament the following November when it reconvened.

On the floor of the House of Commons in 1790, Wilberforce used his oratorical gifts to present the brutalities of the trade: the inhumanity of

---

6. Ibid., 29–30.

how slaves were obtained, the horrors of the Middle Passage (evidenced by the fact that most ship captains put up netting around the side of the ship to prevent the captives from throwing themselves overboard), and the barbarities surviving slaves faced upon their arrival in the West Indies.

Yet while powerful speeches and political alliances made some impact, they did not sway the deeply entrenched commercial interests of the parliamentary representatives. Wilberforce looked to the Clapham Sect to help him switch tactics.

Wilberforce was at first reluctant to engage in what turned out to be a lasting legacy of the campaign: mass mobilization. Clarkson and others had to persuade him to put aside his distrust of "systematic agitation" and go straight to the people. Previous abolitionists had printed Cowper's poem "The Negro's Complaint" on expensive paper, set it to music, and circulated it in fashionable circles. The renown potter Josiah Wedgwood had designed a cameo of a black slave kneeling on a white background with the plea, "Am I not a man and a brother?" This cameo was copied onto snuffboxes and ornamental hairpins and became a fashionable accessory among the elite.[7]

Switching tactics from the elite to the masses, Clarkson set off around the country leaving a trail of activist "corresponding societies" that were ready to organize petitions and try to influence their elected representatives. In addition, Clapham Sect members Thomas Babington and William Smith helped mobilize a boycott of West Indian sugar which, much to Wilberforce's surprise, caught on quickly. In 1792 Clarkson estimated that some three hundred thousand people engaged in it.[8] When in 1792 Wilberforce again introduced his annual motion to abolish the slave trade, he could lay on the table 519 petitions from around the country that supported this movement.

Politics and revolution in Europe brought the movement's increasing momentum to an abrupt halt — if only temporarily. The Reign of Terror following the French Revolution and the 1792 "September Massacre" in Paris horrified the British aristocracy. They began to associate abolition with revolution. Supporters of the slave trade encouraged "gradual" reforms, and popular support waned dramatically.

For more than ten years Wilberforce's annual introduction of anti-slavery bills into the House of Commons met with failure and even

---

7. Ibid., 40.
8. Ibid., 41, quoting *Clarkson's History of Abolition*, 2:349–50.

derision. It was only in 1804, when four of the Clapham Sect had become members of Parliament, when the pall of the French Revolution had subsided and when Parliament saw a dramatic influx of forty abolitionist Irish MPs, that real steps toward progress were taken. Thus eighteen years after he had begun this commitment, Wilberforce's motion to abolish the slave trade passed a first reading of the House of Commons.

Lessons learned

As people of faith taking up the challenge of reducing extreme global poverty and the vast inequalities of resource distribution throughout the world today, we may be tempted, with the benefit of hindsight, to think that the evils of the slave trade were a more obviously "immoral" practice, or an easier target, for religious activism than extreme poverty.

In reality, however, the ignorance, commercial incentives, political interests, and unquestioning acceptance of the status quo in late eighteenth- and early nineteenth-century Britain made the slave trade at least a comparable challenge to reformers then as meeting the MDGs appears to us in the twenty-first century. Like Wilberforce and his compatriots in the Clapham Sect, we need to raise awareness — in our case about both the widespread dehumanizing effects of extreme poverty and our ability to end it. Also, like the nineteenth-century reformers, we must realize that educating elite decision makers is not enough. We need to involve the grass roots.

If the anti-slave-trade campaign teaches us anything, it is that the difficult, systematic work of educating people and amassing political capital is only the beginning of a successful church-led reform campaign. Consumer habits and regulation of business practices may have a greater role in poverty alleviation than the reform of national laws. Who would have thought that any part of the British public could be convinced to give up sugar during Wilberforce's campaign? They did, however, and collectively the boycott made a difference — as did the oxygen of publicity provided by Wedgwood and others. Mobilizing our power as consumers and shareholders, in addition to the support of the well-known and influential, is even more critical today in a world where national and multinational corporations exercise tremendous power.

Divestment from South Africa: The problem

A modern church-based social movement that emphasized shareholder power to advance social change was the anti-apartheid divestment movement the 1960s–80s. Church groups and other non-governmental organizations outside South Africa began to advocate human rights for black, colored, and Asian South Africans who were suffering under apartheid. While political lobbying was one important tactic, religious and secular activists in the United States decided to lobby American companies doing business in South Africa, working in concert with the international community and South Africans themselves. They trusted that the cumulative effect of using economic, moral, cultural, and political tools in isolating the South African government from the rest of the world would dismantle its power inside the country.

In 1970, Timothy Smith, anti-apartheid activist and future founder of the Interfaith Center for Corporate Responsibility, traveled to South Africa. In visiting some two dozen of the sixty-six South African subsidiaries of American companies run by American executives, Smith sought to answer questions often posed by US churches and others: Was the presence of American companies in South Africa helping to end apartheid, or were they bolstering the system? Was there any role that the US business community could play to help end state-sponsored racism, or should American stockholders convince these companies to withdraw from South Africa altogether?

Smith was well aware of what South Africa's apartheid regime meant for more than 16 million black South Africans who made up 69 percent of the country's population. Mirroring the Jim Crow laws of the first half of the twentieth century in the American South, the Afrikaner National Party, which came into power in 1948, introduced apartheid: a racially segregated system which designated blacks and other peoples of color as second-class citizens in their own country. Nonwhites could not vote, could not intermarry, could not form unions, could not be hired for high-paying or skilled work, and were required to carry identity passes while traveling. In addition, black South Africans were restricted to living in "homelands" (with inadequate housing, education, and health care). During a declared state of emergency, such as existed in the late 1980s, nonwhites could be detained for any length of time by the police or military.

While the current system seemed patently unjust to Smith and many others, the precise relationship between American subsidiaries operating in South Africa and the racist regime was less clear. Armed with tape recorders, surveys, and notepads, Smith was surprised by what he discovered during interviews with dozens of American executives living and working in South Africa.[9]

9. These findings are recorded in Robert Massie's book *Loosing the Bonds: The United States and South Africa in the Apartheid Years* (New York: Doubleday, 1997).

While they were consistently cordial and hospitable to him, Smith observed that the South African subsidiaries of American firms seemed almost uniformly to support apartheid's principles. American managers who had harbored bigoted feelings toward American blacks felt the same way about South African blacks. One executive said that black South Africans were "savage";[10] managers of another firm claimed that "Africans lacked reasoning power," "enjoyed repetitive work," and "had no depth perception."[11] Combining paternalism with economic self-interest, Smith further noted, top executives in American companies denied services for black South Africans that would have been considered mandatory in the United States, such as medical insurance, pension plans, or the ability to form labor unions.

During the summer of 1970, overlapping with Smith's fact-finding tour to South Africa, anti-apartheid activists at the General Convention of the Episcopal Church of the United States (ECUSA) introduced a successful resolution asking the presiding bishop, John Hines, to use the Episcopal Church's stocks in General Motors (GM) to pressure the company to the withdraw from South Africa. That winter Hines put the resolution into practice and wrote to the chairman of the board at GM, James M. Roche, warning him that the Episcopal Church was going to use its ownership of 12,574 shares in the company (less than 1 percent of the total number of shares) to offer a resolution urging GM to withdraw from South Africa.

A few months later, to the chagrin of GM's management, Hines made good on his promise and became the first head of a major religious denomination to bring this sort of shareholder resolution to the floor of the annual shareholders' meeting. This resolution was the beginning of the church's shareholder movement that led to the establishment of the Interfaith Council for Corporate Responsibility later that year. It also initiated a larger movement of corporate activism that exists today in response to social injustices ranging from sweatshop labor to environmental devastation.

Bishop Hines, who took the microphone on the floor of GM's 1970 meeting, was no stranger to controversy. Son of a dedicated physician who treated black and white, rich and poor patients alike, Hines grew up in the segregated South in a family that opposed the evils of racism before others in their community. Embracing the social gospel as a young rector in Augusta, Georgia, Hines preached and worked on behalf of

---

10. Ibid., 270.
11. Ibid.

African Americans who lived in tenements, attended inferior schools, and held low-paying jobs.[12] This commitment continued when Hines became presiding bishop; in the summer of 1967, following race riots in cities across America, Hines persuaded the national church to put one-sixth of its budget toward alleviating poverty and furthering civil rights in America's inner cities. An allocation of $200,000 from its current budget and $2 million for the following three years (almost one sixth of the entire church's budget) in no-strings-attached funding for America's cities, Hines argued, was a step in line with the Christian gospel. Unlike his opponents, Hines felt that this transfer of resources did not represent a "perpetualization of the institution through which the Gospel is transmitted."[13] Many disagreed.

The leap from domestic poverty and racism in America's cities to the injustices of the apartheid regime in South Africa was a small one for Hines. During the decades that followed the historic shareholder resolution, the divestment movement in America grew in size and diversity. Other church leaders joined a growing chorus of secular and faith-based organizations shocked by the racist policies of South Africa's apartheid government and willing to challenge America's engagement with it. By 1980, when Ronald Reagan was elected to the White House and made it clear that neither divestment nor sanctions would be part of the US government's official policy, the president faced an increasingly vocal group of religious and secular activists, led by the prophetic voices of religious opposition to apartheid within South Africa itself.

One way that the anti-apartheid divestment movement in the United States differed profoundly from the anti-slave-trade campaign in Britain over a century and a half earlier was that reformers took their lead and direction from the voices of the oppressed — South Africans on whose behalf they advocated. Theological and political action plans included the Harare Declaration, a 1985 statement that demanded international sanctions against South Africa, and the Kairos Document (1987), which denounced apartheid. Both documents were drafted by South African religious leaders with input from international activists and foreign church officials. They provided a blueprint for action among international religious bodies determined to support their brothers' and sisters' struggles on the inside.

---

12. Kenneth Kesselus, " 'Awake, Thou Spirit of the Watchmen,' John E. Hines's Challenge to the Episcopal Church," *Anglican and Episcopal History* 64, no. 3 (1995): 303.

13. Ibid., 311.

Of all the South African religious voices that spurred American activists, that of Desmond Tutu, Nobel laureate and the Anglican archbishop of Cape Town, was among the most stirring. According to Nelson Mandela, "Sometimes strident, often tender, never afraid, and seldom without humor, Desmond Tutu's voice will always be the voice of the voiceless."[14]

Archbishop Tutu was unequivocal in his criticism of gradualism — then called "constructive engagement." In his view, the Sullivan Code (which was adopted by 145 American companies) that called on American companies to remain in the country and advocate "desegregation of the work place, fair employment practices, equal pay for equal work, job training and advancement, and improvement in the quality of workers' lives" was simply a means "to help make apartheid more acceptable, more comfortable." As he said, "we do not want apartheid made more comfortable, we want apartheid dismantled."[15]

In 1986 Archbishop Tutu went a step further and called for international sanctions against South Africa. Quoting a 1985 poll conducted by the *Sunday Times* of London that 77 percent of urban blacks in South Africa supported sanctions, and calling the Reagan policy of constructive engagement a failure, Archbishop Tutu drew a line in the sand that helped create momentum for change inside the US churches and beyond. With his clear call for specific actions, Tutu quickened the pace of change.

Inside the Episcopal Church and a number of other denominations, 1986 was a watershed year. The vestry of Trinity Church, Wall Street, voted to divest all of its holdings in companies doing business in South Africa, which amounted to $10 million and 20 percent of the stock portfolio of one of the most well-endowed parishes in America. Other parishes, dioceses, and seminaries followed suit. Also in 1986, fifteen years after Bishop Hines introduced the anti-apartheid resolution at GM's shareholder meeting, this leading company sold all its South African assets.

Momentum for divestment gathered outside the church as well. In October 1986, overriding a presidential veto, Congress passed the Comprehensive Anti-Apartheid Act. This law halted the domestic sale of Krugerrands; ended flights between South Africa and the US; banned import of iron, steel, uranium, coal, textiles, and agricultural products; and barred American firms from making any new investments in South Africa.

---

14. Cited in Dave Andrews, "People of Faith: Desmond Tutu," *Target* (Tearfund) 3 (2004), *www.tear.org.au/resources/target/051/13.people-of-faith.htm.*

15. Cited in Manning Marable, "The Case for Divestment," *The Witness* 68, no. 6 (June 1985): 8–10.

Imprisoned by Hope

The former South African archbishop Desmond Tutu used to famously say, "We are prisoners of hope." Such a statement might be taken as merely rhetorical or even eccentric if you hadn't seen Bishop Tutu stare down the notorious South African security police when they broke into the Cathedral of St. George's during his sermon at an ecumenical service. I was there.... The incident taught me more about the power of hope than any other moment in my life. Desmond Tutu stopped preaching and just looked at the intruders as they lined the walls of his cathedral, wielding writing pads and tape recorders to record whatever he said and thereby threatening him with consequences for any bold prophetic utterances. They had already arrested Tutu and other church leaders just a few weeks before and kept them in jail for several days to make both a statement and a point: Religious leaders who take on leadership roles in the struggle against apartheid will be treated like any other opponents of the Pretoria regime.

After meeting their eyes with his in a steely gaze, the church leader acknowledged their power ("you are powerful, very powerful") but reminded them that he served a higher power greater than their political authority ("But I serve a God who cannot be mocked!"). Then, in the most extraordinary challenge to political tyranny I have ever witnessed, Archbishop Desmond Tutu told the representatives of South African apartheid, "Since you have already lost, I invite you today to come and join the winning side!" He said it with a smile on his face and enticing warmth in his invitation, but with a clarity and boldness that took everyone's breath away. The congregation's response was electric. The crowd was literally transformed by the bishop's challenge to power. From a cowering fear of the heavily armed security forces that surrounded the cathedral and greatly outnumbered the band of worshipers, we literally leaped to our feet, shouted the praises of God and began... dancing. (What is it about dancing that enacts and embodies the spirit of hope?) We danced out of the cathedral to meet the awaiting police and military forces of apartheid who hardly expected a confrontation with dancing worshipers. Not knowing what else to do, they backed up to provide the space for the people of faith to dance for freedom in the streets of South Africa.

— Jim Wallis, *God's Politics: Why the Right Gets It Wrong and the Left Doesn't Get It* (San Francisco: HarperSanFrancisco, 2005), 348.

It also linked the alleviation of these restrictions to conditions like the release of Nelson Mandela. That same year, the University of California sold $3.1 billion in stocks and bonds of companies with South African involvement, and a few months later three major pension plans in the state of California, together worth $65 billion, divested from companies doing business there. Finally, culturally and psychologically, white South Africa was becoming isolated from the global community: American musicians refused to play at Sun City in 1985, and films like *Master Harold and the Boys* and the increasingly frosty reception that white South Africans had as they traveled abroad added to a sense of isolation from the world community.[16]

In less than three years the situation in South Africa changed drastically. The combined pressures of international sanctions, the outflow of capital and investment (from January 1986 until April 1988, 114 US companies pulled out of South Africa), and cultural isolation had a stunning and swift effect. By 1989 the hardline leader of the National Party, President P. W. Botha, was out of office. A year later the new, more moderate President F. W. De Klerk had lifted the ban on the African National Congress (ANC) and other opposition parties, ended emergency rule, and on February 7, 1990, released Nelson Mandela from prison on Robben Island, where he had served twenty-seven years. It was another four years of hard-fought negotiations and sporadic violence in townships and elsewhere before Nelson Mandela was elected South Africa's first nonwhite president in the country's first all-race democratic election in 1994. Over 90 percent of adult South Africans voted, many for the first time in their lives.

Jim Wallis writes that "hope is believing despite the evidence, and then watching the evidence change."[17] As we recall the example of faithful activists and saints of the past and their example of courage, optimism, determination, and perseverance, it gives us hope in our work for poverty reduction. Like them we will face doubts, and we may at times grow weary and despondent, but their example shows us what can be done — *what one person can do* — in the face of seemingly intractable problems. Often, it is people of faith who provide that energy for social transformation.

---

16. Massie, *Loosing the Bonds*, 632.
17. Jim Wallis, "The Power of Hope: A Sign of Transformation," *Sojourners Magazine* (September–October 1994).

?? QUESTIONS FOR DISCUSSION

Go back through this chapter and think about the people who made courageous decisions and who worked, on and off, for years and years to bring about a change:

◆ William Wilberforce, who made abolition his life's work — the law passed eighteen years after he proposed it.

◆ Timothy Smith, who documented and publicized the complicity of American firms with apartheid.

◆ Bishop Hines, who took the microphone at a General Motors meeting — fifteen years before GM withdrew.

◆ Archbishop Tutu, who gave clear direction to oppose gradualism, to divest, and to impose sanctions.

◆ Vestry members of Trinity Church, Wall Street, who together decided to divest.

◆ Political representatives, who together passed anti-apartheid legislation over a presidential veto.

Each of these individuals or groups, with other priorities in their lives, made a difference. Do any of these examples capture your attention? What is it that intrigues you?

Lessons learned

What else does the South African liberation struggle teach us? Again, the challenge seemed intractable, and indeed the struggle took over fifteen years. A few people made significant contributions. It took time to raise awareness, to build consensus and support. But once this was achieved, the movement took root and generated considerable momentum. Very specific actions were identified that individuals and churches could do. In hindsight, leaders who were once treated with caution and suspicion became saints and heroes.

The two examples in this chapter are indeed stories to inspire. They also provide pragmatic lessons of history, as each generation learns from and builds on the past. So often the cumulative effect of the efforts of individuals and groups builds the momentum to achieve the seemingly impossible. It is not out of place to recall words used in a rather different context by the great scientist Sir Isaac Newton, one person who transformed scientific thought. He realized that he was part of a much greater scientific movement and was indebted to those who had gone before when he said, "If I have seen further it is by standing on the shoulders of giants."[18] Those working for social justice today can see further when they likewise stand on giants' shoulders.

MDGs

Goal 5: Improve maternal health

Women's needs are implicit in all the MDGs, as it is women who constitute the majority of the poor and who are most often affected by problems such as water shortages, the hunger and illness of children and families, and so on. However, Goal 3, which was discussed earlier, and this goal are focused on two needs that are particular to women. Specifically, Goal 5 is to reduce by three-quarters, between 1990 and 2015, the maternal mortality ratio.

Worldwide, more than 50 million women suffer from poor reproductive health and serious pregnancy-related illnesses and disabilities. And every year more than 500,000 women die from complications of pregnancy and childbirth — most in Sub-Saharan Africa. In fact, more women die in childbirth annually than all the people who die in wars (in 2003, an estimated 179,000 people died in war). We may think of births as occasions of joy, but many women are fearful during pregnancy, afraid they may die as they bring forth life.

Why do mothers die?

Mothers die because of hemorrhages, infections, hypertension, and obstructed labor. The primary way to prevent mothers' deaths is to provide rapid access to emergency obstetrical care by having a midwife or doctor present at delivery. Right now across the developing countries, 42 percent of mothers give birth without a midwife or doctor present.

How are we doing so far?

Only 17 percent of all developing countries are on target to reduce maternal mortality by three-quarters before 2015. South Asia is in the worst position — only 21 percent of all women have trained midwives or doctors present when they give birth, and among the poor this drops to 7 percent. However, South Asia is making strong progress. Among the poor in Sub-Saharan Africa and Latin America 25 percent and 44 percent of births are attended, respectively,

---

18. Letter to Robert Hooke, February 5, 1675.

but maternal mortality appears to be increasing, which is cause for considerable concern.

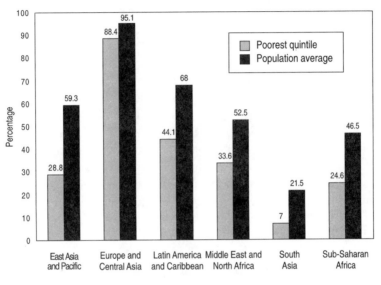

Frequency of attended births by wealth and region

Source: "Global Monitoring Report 2004: Policies and Actions for Achieving the Millennium Development Goals and Related Outcomes" (Washington, D.C.: World Bank, 2004), Table 7.3, p. 119, based on USAID data.

ACTION 7:
GET POLITICAL — ADVOCATE!

Working toward reducing global poverty is not a top political priority. In comparison with domestic concerns, issues relating to the MDGs receive little attention on the floor of the US Congress, or in committee hearings or press statements. The British Parliament recently has given these greater visibility — particularly because of the Blair Commission for Africa and Gordon Brown's involvement in the International Finance Facility. Yet in both countries, the rhetoric about global poverty exceeds the level of commitment.

This action asks you to take the time to write your elected representative on Overseas Development Assistance and the Millennium Development Goals. It asks you to consider meeting with your representative and expressing your support for the MDGs and for increased ODA, fairer trade, and deeper debt relief in your local newspaper.

Why and how your letter works — the plain facts

Heads of state, members of Parliament, US representatives, and US senators receive staggering amounts of mail, phone calls, faxes, and e-mail from their constituents every day. Most rarely read individual pieces of general constituent mail. But your letter still counts — literally — as do e-mails and phone calls. Your representative will most likely never see your letter. What he or she probably will see, however, is a daily or weekly tally of how many letters, e-mails, and calls have been received on different issues and whether or not constituents are "pro" or "con." This tally can affect the questions a representative asks, the bills a representative cosponsors, and how he or she votes. So, yes, you might be just a number, but numbers matter. Timing does too. Having a few people e-mail or phone on the same day (perhaps during the church coffee hour) makes for a more striking tally than if someone phoned every few days over a month.

Writing an effective letter

Good letters matter. Apparently when the Save the Children Fund in Britain surveyed MPs to identify what raised MPs' own awareness of campaigns, they found that personal letters were twenty-six times more effective than general media coverage.[19] Here are some things you can do to increase the chances that your letter or e-mail will be read as well as counted.

The first rule is to confirm that you are a constituent and include your postal mailing address as proof. Senators, representatives, and MPs rarely respond to individuals outside of their district (or in the case of a senator, outside of their state). Including your full postal address is important, even if you are sending an e-mail, as many legislative offices still respond by regular mail.

The second is to be personal and specific. Write about someone you've met from a developing country, your work overseas, or a program undertaken by your church. Provide vivid examples of how ODA has made a difference. If possible, mention other local friends or area groups (who will also be the legislator's constituents) who share your concern about global poverty.

---

19. *www.christianaid.org.uk/campaign/resource/0301lwg.htm*, accessed February 8, 2005.

Be specific about what you are asking the representative to do, such as vote for passage of a specific bill or amendment or resolution, or press for increased appropriations for existing programs or authorization for new ones. Remember that your correspondence will be of more value if you write before a critical vote. Many antipoverty organizations as well as denominational government relations offices offer e-mail notification services to alert members about impending legislation.

Other things to remember:

* Be polite and brief (one page should do).

* Do not carbon copy excessively. This may make a response less likely.

* Do not spam. If you write every day, it's unlikely that you will be taken seriously. (You might even wind up in a so-called STUN file — that's NUTS spelled backward.)

* Thank the member if he or she votes as you hoped.

A strong letter will not guarantee a personal response, but it does raise the odds that your letter will bring the concerns of global poverty to your representative. As the Conservative MP Caroline Spelman, speaking as opposition spokesperson on International Development in the UK, said, "It is essential that constituents raise development issues with their MPs, as it ensures that we hear the voice of the world's poor amongst all the competing attention of needs closer to home."[20]

Politicians also read newspapers and accept visitors

The media also influence politicians. All politicians track what is being said about them by name in the news far more intently than they follow media coverage of issues such as the MDGs. Most offices have a press intern who dutifully clips out all references to the representative in major national news outlets as well as local newspapers. This includes letters to the editor and op-eds. The politician can review the clips daily. It is a political reality that if you write a short, well-argued opinion piece in a local newspaper, it will likely carry far more weight than a general press release offered by national church leaders or global antipoverty agency. Why not try it out?

In addition, most MPs and US representatives visit their home constituency regularly and have an office there. You can make an appointment, get a small group together, prepare and practice your presentation and request, and present these compelling issues in person.

---

20. Ibid.

What Happens to Your Letter?

To give you a little idea of why your letter matters, we're going to sketch out the typical mail process for a constituent letter to the US Senate.

The letter arrives (after being irradiated to reduce the threat of anthrax contamination) at the senator's front office. The mail is then sorted and coded by interns, staff assistants, or a mail coordinator — sometimes by all three. If it's about an issue that the senator has already received a lot of mail on, chances are there is already a form letter on that subject with which they will respond to you. Actually, there are probably two form letters — one "pro" and one "con" — depending on whether or not the constituent (you) has voiced support or opposition to a particular policy. Your letter would be put in a batch with similar letters and sent to the printing office to receive the appropriate form letter.

The remaining letters are sorted as either a *case* or an *issue*. A *case* is a constituent who needs help. *Issue* letters raise questions or concerns regarding a particular policy area (e.g., the MDGs). Issue letters are assigned to a young legislative correspondent (LC) whose job is to answer letters relating to certain issues. If the LC doesn't know how to answer a particular letter, he or she will usually ask a senior advisor. When the LC is finished, an advisor or mail editor may check the letter before it's printed and sent to the autopen, which will confer the senator's signature. The incoming constituent letter will then be filed, and the senator's outgoing response will be saved in a mail database that tracks all of the senator's constituent correspondence.

This sounds all rather procedural and cold, but it is a route by which elected representatives **do** try to stay informed in between elections, and to communicate their own views and actions.

Useful Web sites on letter-writing

The following are only a small assortment of Christian groups in the US and UK who ask Christians to write letters related to the MDGs, and inform them how to do so in a constructive and timely manner. Many of them have "e-mail alerts" you can sign up for so you will be informed just prior to an important vote. It takes one to five minutes to respond to each alert.

Advocacy in the US — useful Web sites

The Church World Service posts e-mail action alerts. Sign up at *http://capwiz.com/ churchworld/home/*. It also links to a number of advocacy organizations by theme. Visit *www.churchworldservice.org/Educ_Advo/links.html*.

The Episcopal Public Policy Network (*www.episcopalchurch.org/eppn/*) e-mails policy alerts (usually two or three a month) on a variety of legislative matters, including foreign aid and policy, to subscribers. EPPN runs a grassroots advocacy network which can assist advocates in contacting their representatives.

Many other groups run e-mail action alerts — for example:

www.bread.org/issues/ONE_campaign/take_action provides information about Bread for the World and the ONE Campaign, a US campaign focused on the MDGs. The Web site includes a section called "Write to Congress."

DATA: *www.data.org/action/* gives information for phoning your representative toll-free.

World Vision: *www.worldvision.org/worldvision/wvususfo.nsf/stable/globalissues_action*

Sojourners: *www.sojo.net/action,* (an evangelical social justice alliance working on domestic and international US matters)

Faithful America: *www.faithfulamerica.org/Action.htm,* an ecumenical progressive alliance for political activism.

Maryknoll Office of Global Concerns (*www.maryknollogc.org*): Action Alerts inform visitors about global issues and pending legislation.

US Catholic Grassroots Advocacy: *www.catholicrelief.org/get_involved/advocacy/grass_roots/ index.cfm*.

United Methodists: *http://capwiz.com/gbcs/home/*.

THOMAS: *http://thomas.loc.gov* offers information on federal legislation, including bill summary and status, and the text of the Congressional Record.

Oxfam: *secure.ga3.org/02/oxfamamerica* undertakes advocacy on diverse issues.

Care USA: *www.careusa.org/getinvolved/* offers action alerts, as well as volunteer opportunities and other ways to get involved.

Advocacy in the UK — useful Web sites

www.locata.co.uk/commons gives contact details of MPs.

www.christian-aid.org.uk/campaign gives information on Christian Aid's "Sponsored by Letters" campaign on trade justice. It is a strong first port of call for all advocacy work.

www.oxfam.org.uk likewise is a leading voice for advocacy in the UK.

www.cafod.org.uk/resources includes a section called "How to Lobby your MP."

www.tearfund.org/Campaigning includes "A Guide to Working with your MP."

8

The Spirit of Social Justice

Elusive Dawn

Mahbub ul Haq, the Pakistani economist whose vision, eloquence, political sense, and determination gave rise to the Human Development Reports of the United Nations, was also a poet. Not only did he lead others in crafting the Human Development Index, which compares countries not according to income but according to their people's well-being; he also penned this translation of the poem "Elusive Dawn" by the great Urdu poet Faiz Ahmed Faiz.

This trembling light, this night-bitten Dawn
This is not the Dawn we awaited for so long
This is not the Dawn whose birth was sired
By so many lives, by so much blood.
       Generations ago, we started our confident march,
       Our hopes were young, our goal within reach.
After all, there must be some limit
To the confusing constellation of stars
In the vast forest of the sky.
Even the lazy, languid waves
Must reach at last their appointed shore.
       And so we wistfully prayed
       For a consummate end to our painful search
       Many a temptation crossed our forbidden path;
       Many inviting bodies; many longing arms
       Many seductive pleasures beckoned us on the way.
But we stayed faithful to our distant dream
We kept marching to a different drum,
We kept searching for our lost freedom,
We kept looking for our elusive Dawn.
       We are told: your new Dawn is already here;
       Your tired feet need journey no more.
       Our rulers whisper seductively:
       Why this constant struggle? Why this perpetual search?

Come, join us, enjoy this new-found wealth
Built by the toil of our "liberated" poor.
And yet, even today,
Our hearts are aflame,
Our desires unquenched,
Our goals unmet.
Was there a streak of light?
Where did it go?
The wayside lamp just blinked unawares.
This is yet no relief in the darkness of the Night;
No liberation yet of our soul and minds.
So let us keep marching, my tiring friends:
We have yet to find our elusive Dawn.

— Faiz 'Subah Azadi,' *Daste Saba* (trans. Mahbub ul Haq.)

Working for poverty reduction can be dangerous. Because the task is so important, so urgent, it can dominate our lives. Sometimes we feel as though we have truly found our calling and that we are able to give our lives and energies to something that really matters. At other times our commitments to reducing impoverishment create resistance, self-righteousness, panic, frustration, despair, or disillusionment. Sometimes they crowd God out of the center of our lives. Sometimes they make us mad at God or disappointed in God, such as when we confront persistent injustice, suffering, or the church's inactivity.

Throughout this book we have suggested that living with this tension — between recurring human suffering and our consistent emphatic duty to respond — is something Christians can learn to do well. We argue that small actions within busy lives are enough. But some people choose more extensive engagement. This last chapter explores the spirituality that emerges when poverty reduction becomes a significant priority, and suggests some spiritual resources that can support a healthy and enduring response. It shows how working for poverty reduction, at whatever level of commitment, can deepen our spiritual lives and renew us and, through us, God's church.

Dealing with failures and celebrating successes, even when they are incomplete and transitory, is important to do well and faithfully. Campaigns arise and decline. We never quite know which one will make a lasting difference. People join social movements like the MDG campaign and leave them again. Even the MDGs are imperfect and incomplete.

Moreover we have no idea for how long world leaders will pay attention to them. But the principles for which the MDGs imperfectly stand are enduring, and the God who yearns for justice will *not* abandon them.

A spiritual journey

How can we make our response to poverty endure year in and year out? One way is to understand a bit more the spiritual terrain along the path of social commitment, for the pursuit of justice can nurture our relationship with God in different ways. In this chapter we are going to identify certain features that recur in different people's journeys, with the hope that awareness of these features will enable others to stop and refresh themselves along the way.

You might have heard of the stages of grief, aptly described by Elisabeth Kübler-Ross. Her writings have enabled many bereaved people to understand their experiences of shock, denial, anger, sadness, and acceptance — and to understand and empathize with others as they go through them. Or, in your prayer life, you may have had a range of experiences, from times when God seems distressingly absent, to times of overwhelming joy, when you feel you are under the waterfall of God's love. Spiritual writers such as Teresa of Ávila or John of the Cross describe these experiences as "stages of contemplation." Everyone's journey of faith is distinctive, but there are patterns, and we gain self-understanding when we recognize them.

There are common spiritual experiences too for those who take the path of social justice. We will use the term "social justice" instead of "poverty reduction" during this chapter, because this material might apply not only to poverty reduction but also to confronting racism or other social injustices. Our experiences come in different orders, in different ways, sometimes repeatedly, some not at all, as everyone's journey is robustly unique. Yet some general waymarks can be identified. For shorthand purposes only we will call them "phases" or "stages." Anticipation of these enables us to look out for certain features, to look forward to what may lie ahead, to understand others who are at a different phase, and to enjoy the task at hand.

Reflecting on the experiences of people of various faiths who have devoted much of their time and energy to work for poverty reduction, five important "spiritual phases of engagement" in social justice or poverty reduction stand out. At various times these can become the spiritual driving force of their work. They are the following:

- a strong sense of compassion for those in need (*compassion*)

- a strong sense of responsibility for the plight of the poor (*responsibility*)

- a strong sense of respect for the poor as our equals before God (*respect*)

- a strong sense of peace with the limits and importance of our work (*humility*)

- a strong sense of dependence on God to bring all efforts to fruition (*dependence*)

The questions faced in each phase remain constant: How do we remain faithful to God? How do we use the experience to grow closer to God? How do we integrate social justice work with other commitments? How do we keep the faith when we "fail" and suffering increases? How do we stay engaged when we "succeed" yet we know there is more to do? How do we sustain the work when it is boring and mundane? Maturity in a life of social justice oddly (or perhaps not so oddly) mirrors maturity in the spiritual life, for it entails a deep shift from reliance on oneself to reliance on God. The five phases of social commitment help us to make that shift in different ways. Thinking even briefly about phases helps us understand some of the ways that commitments and ideas evolve, and how different emotions, reactions, and spiritual insights come into focus more strongly at some times than others.

A slightly unexpected benefit of understanding these phases is that they can help us relate better to those working alongside us. In fact, the phases above were identified by field staff in a small development agency. They were of various ages and faiths, and some were not religious at all. However, they wanted to understand and affirm the distinctive perspectives and motivations that were present within the team and identify sources of tension. These phases emerged from their observations.

Their experience of team tension is not uncommon, for in truth, other people can be a strain — even if they are friends, they share our faith, or are very devoted to the cause. Remarkably, the number one reason that committed, dedicated, prayerful Christians *leave* mission work earlier than they planned is *other missionaries*. They couldn't get along with each other. And so we have to learn to support people in various phases, to learn from them, to regard them with wonder, and will their good. Sometimes this seems a far more perplexing task than social justice work itself. But if we draw back from working together, we will go back to each being "just one person," not the collective force for good described in chapter 6. If for no other reason than to address poverty effectively (and there are other good reasons as well), we have to learn to work with those who are different from us. Understanding the phases described in this chapter can help us do that.

Compassion

Compassion wakes when our eyes turn and focus on what is the lived experience of extreme poverty. Maybe compassion is awakened by a vivid talk about poverty. Maybe you see a graphic, even hideous, exposé of human rights abuses — or read an article about child soldiers. Maybe you travel and see a begging toddler with your own eyes, and there was no one to censor the truth. Maybe compassion is stirred by a television program or a movie, and you recognize as if for the first time how much more you have than another. Something awakens us to others' experiences, and we discover our capacity to suffer with others.

The beauty of this phase is that it exercises people's love in such a way that their capacity to love expands. Many, even most, people who ask God, "What can I do?" ask this question because someone's story touched their heart. This question has gained more immediacy as opportunities for travel have opened our eyes to the wider world.

People respond to the awakening of compassion in different ways. Sometimes they wish to stir others' compassion, and so write or give sermons or slide shows in order to share their experience. Often they feel compelled to pray and lift up this situation in their personal prayers, or add them to intercessions in church. Perhaps they give some money or write letters — anything to help. Sometimes they make a radical commitment and change their lifestyle. Often they question the plausibility of a loving God who could allow such suffering. In fact, they respond in many of the ways discussed in this book.

Sometimes they are able to connect with others through experiences of suffering in their own lives, and yet reach out as "wounded healers." The idea of the wounded healer is simple yet profound. Someone who has been wounded — perhaps by an illness, homelessness, penury, bereavement, or the breakdown of a relationship — may be especially able and motivated to support others in a similar situation. A wounded healer may have special insights and be able to empathize with those who suffer.

How does our compassion deepen our relationship with God? One way is to take human suffering into God's presence in prayer. Take, for example, the nun we have already referred to who listens avidly to radio news. After listening she takes troubling stories into what she calls "the crossing point." The crossing point is the intersection between all the pain we inflict on one another and find all around us in humanity — and the presence of God. Her vocation is to stay in this swirling intersection and pray; to stay with the reality of human cruelty and insensitivity and power — to look at it, to listen to it in the news, to allow the pain and anger and hollow despair of people affected to enter into her being, and then in prayer to ask the transforming love of God to meet them and to make them whole. She does that every day. In Action 1, on prayer, we asked you to join her from time to time.

In this phase, as in each of the others, it is also possible for the experience of compassion to be misunderstood and to become a place from which we never move on. Or it can be a dead end. One exhausting dead end is to think that grief is sufficient. If a story on the news makes you feel sad enough, if it keeps you awake at night and if you weep when you remember it, you might think that your response epitomizes compassion. Weeping itself can be a spiritual expression. Yet at some point we need to let the feelings motivate us to act.

Another temptation is simply to evade tough situations that require compassion. When people have been recently bereaved or divorced, they often complain that even close friends avoid them. Their suffering makes friends feel helpless and inadequate, afraid they will say something stupid. Ironically, their friends' silence merely compounds their suffering. Similarly, people are afraid to learn about the pain of impoverishment for fear that they will not be able to do anything useful in response. But as this book argues throughout, we can.

Another temptation is to cultivate an impenetrable protective shell — a barrier that permits no pain in nor allows any expression of pain out. For compassion, which literally means "suffering with," hurts. Emotions can embarrass. Some people are unable to shut out shocking images, and feel tormented by them. They may feel guilty, bereft, or powerless. When compassion has a paralyzing effect it is natural to think that in order to endure in this work one has learn to stifle one's emotions and become inured to others' pain. Naturally some protective shells will form. Yet we must also allow compassion to be rekindled again and again.

This phase of compassion, although the first to be described, is an advanced expression of love. For consideration has stretched beyond the self, beyond the circle of family and friends, beyond the larger circle of work, or neighborhood, or nation, to encounter other vulnerable persons who are beloved of God. So while it may be a painful stage, the pain comes because our love has extended — as God requires and as God's own love does.

Responsibility

In the second phase, our eyes turn to human action. We grasp that we and others *can* act, and that our actions matter. To do nothing could be not merely suboptimal but wrong. God could, in this case, judge us and condemn our unresponsiveness. This is the phase of justice — when people argue that we would be culpable before God and each other if we *failed* to respond to the impoverished.

In this phase people undertake actions that at once please God and serve others. They analyze the structures of sin — ranging from unfair trade policies and debt burdens, to imbalanced spending priorities or poor environmental protocols and labor conditions in their own businesses and corporations. They raise awareness. They campaign. They network. They cry out. In this phase people realize that in order for policies and institutions to change, many have to act. So they try to persuade others to join in the work. This is, as you can imagine, a very evangelical phase.

The beauty of this phase is that people have moved into being laborers in some sense; they have taken hold of their talents and asked how best to use them. They are willing to allow God to hold them accountable for their actions, and willing to use their time, money, and gifts in the ways God requires, indeed to be coworkers with Christ. "Coworkers" is a term that Mother Teresa used for the men and women who volunteer alongside her sisters and brothers. Coworkers join their energies, labors, and love with God's, and in doing so advance the mission of God.

How might this sense of responsibility, accountability, and justice deepen our relationship with God? Sometimes people tap into God's longing: how God yearns for their actions of service. They may become acutely aware of God's plea for faithful people to act on behalf of justice. And they may become aware, even if dimly, that God is present in their work.

Such a rich stage is bound to have a panoply of hazards. One is to think that our work is so important, and so much of God, that we do not need a life of worship and prayer, and that service is enough. It is at this stage that some people leave the institutional church, because they have found the love they sought enacted more forcefully among activists and servants of the poor than among priests and Bible study groups. "This is my worship," they may say, feeding a malnourished baby or writing a newspaper article about a refugee family. Their words should be heard as a legitimate challenge to the churches. Yet rightly done, worship and prayer can nourish, deepen, and even complement immediate action.

Another overwhelming temptation of this stage is to be so concerned and committed to a particular goal or set of goals that we become shrill, pushy, and obsessive. Such people view their cause as so terribly important and urgent that they seem unbearably zealous. They do not pause to separate their work from their very being, but talk about their cause, bully others to attend meetings, and hand out their pamphlets at every occasion. Often others condemn such people for having messiah complexes, or for needing desperately to be needed. Yet what might also be occurring at this stage is that people are learning how much power they have to effect change or to persuade others and discerning how much God asks of them. They are also trying to be willing to respond to everything God requires — even if it is social ostracism. They are trying to mature in love and to give more. Naturally all of us go wrong many times, but if we keep trying and keep listening, God will guide us.

Other people's advice or condemnation is, at this stage, not necessarily an accurate guide. Sometimes the pressure that we put on others can be socially awkward, and they object. Like judgmental prophets, there are moments when we bellow. It's not always pretty. But at times — like Jesus' confrontation in the temple, turning tables upside down — it may be the only faithful thing to do.

A good example of this is Bob Geldof, whose anger at the starvation deaths of Ethiopian children mentioned in chapter 5 propelled him to become a John-the-Baptist-like prophetic voice. Bob Geldof was an unlikely hero — even to himself. As *Life* magazine put it in a Geldof-like way, "Did God knock at the wrong door by mistake and, when it was opened by this scruffy Irishman, think, 'Oh, what the hell — he'll do' "?[1] Disheveled, prone to uttering expletives, Geldof mixed compassion, outrage, and determination into a compelling cocktail.

Prophetic leadership, action, and voice are really very important to the church and to society at large. People who have embraced their responsibilities and are encouraging, insisting, commanding that others take responsibility for their actions may be regarded as a nuisance — which is not a label anyone seeks. Yet without stubborn determination it is really easy for things to be left undone — in churches and in wider circles. If we are convinced a situation is unjust, we must allow ourselves again and again to chafe against it, and remind ourselves of responsibilities that we are not fulfilling. We will talk in the last section about how to strike a healthy balance between these conflicting priorities.

---

1. Cited in "Do They Know It's 20 Years Ago?" *Times* (London), October 23, 2004. Online at *www.timesonline.co.uk/article/0,,7948-1323842,00.html.*

?? **QUESTION FOR DISCUSSION**

◆ When have you "bellowed" or taken a prophetic role? How did it feel?
   How did you know whether you were doing the right thing?

Respect

Another phase arises when our eyes turn to the people we are trying to
"help." We realize that we are responding not to an amorphous and de-
personalized entity, "the poor," but to lively human beings with names
and stories and favorite meals and senses of humor. This can be a sudden
apprehension. We see, often with a start and a flood of shame or embarrassment, that we have, hitherto, ignored them. We have spoken of these
people as "poor" and urged others to "respond." But we have thought
of the impoverished mainly as suffering victims of circumstance. Then
we notice they are real people. Furthermore we grasp that in the long
term sustained poverty reduction will not occur unless they are among
the primary actors, unless they are in the driver's seat.

This, too, is a beautiful phase. It is a phase of repentance for past
wrongs inflicted by well-intentioned persons. It is a phase in which relationships with "the poor" gradually deepen. A seminarian who visited
Ethiopia — a poor, war-torn, and famine-prone country — was very startled when he met Ethiopians. For he found that poorly dressed, thin
Ethiopians were actually proud of their country, with its ancient roots
and delicious coffee, and were articulate about their own situation. Their
posture did not match the "poor Ethiopian" he had expected to meet,
and he had to adjust swiftly his understanding of "the poor."

Development, relief, and mission agencies of the churches have, one by
one, passed through a similar deliberate maturation and transformation.
Whereas once they spoke of beneficiaries, now they speak of partners.
Whereas once their posters showed emaciated children with tragic eyes,
now posters depict energetic poor men and women and children building
their lives together. Whereas even recently missionary and development
agencies presumed a privileged voice and authority in decision making,
now their leaders are invited on immersion courses to meet the poor
(see Action 4), and their partners in turn challenge paternalism and take
leadership.

People in this phase focus on mutuality and respect. They slice away pretensions of Western leaders "solving" world poverty and become, for a time, dogmatic about "empowering" the others.

The temptation in this phase as in others is to withdraw entirely from "helping" (which is now deemed patronizing) and disengage. At times some feel it would be better if all "development" groups went home, because in aiming to help they have made such a muddle of things. Other times the disengagement is fueled by resentment. People are often surprised by the resilience and creativity of poor communities. They are equally taken aback if they encounter antagonism — as the church ladies did to their collection of garden hoes in chapter 4 — or if they witness people's resentment of historical oppressions.

When we realize that poor people are not necessarily docile hero-worshipers, the pendulum may swing and we cynically wish them to be entirely independent and find grassroots solutions to all difficulties. But this will not work. We have more than our share of wealth; the policies made by our elected representatives can and do wreak havoc; and even our own skills may be of service. It is healthy to realize that our actions, while crucial, will not be sufficient, and to recognize that our powers — however considerable and necessary — are incomplete without the enthusiastic leadership of poor persons and of local leaders. Yet to indulge in cynicism and inaction would be culpably negligent.

The spiritual potential of this stage may be to encounter God, who is at once active and entirely beyond our control. It is an odd and awesome liberation when we glimpse the extent of God's concerns and those of God's people. Max Warren, a former general secretary of the Church Missionary Society, reminded Christians working in other faith contexts, "Our first task in approaching another people . . . is to take off our shoes, for the place we are approaching is holy; else we may find ourselves treading on someone's dreams. More serious still, we may forget that God was there before our arrival."[2] Similarly, we may grasp God is *already* at work, in and through not only the Western "helpers," but in other religious and service organizations and governments, as well as in the "victims" and the "beneficiaries." And we may adore the God who is greater than we often acknowledge and has resources of which we know not.

In the phase of responsibility, the question is, "What can I do?" In the phase of respect, the questions are, "How should I relate?" and "How

2. Max Warren, in the introduction to Kenneth Cragg, *Sandals at the Mosque: Christian Presence amid Islam* (London: SCM Press, 1959), 9–10. Max Warren was the general secretary of the Church Missionary Society (CMS) in the UK from 1942 to 1962.

can I respond to and 'serve' the impoverished with mature respect and liberating mutuality?" It is also, in this phase, that we realize so keenly that material poverty may go alongside spiritual and relational wisdom and ripeness that we do not have. So the relationships we kindle come to be genuine and mutually enriching.

?? QUESTIONS FOR DISCUSSION

- ◆ In your work or in your travels, have you had any surprises like the seminarian? How do you view the poor now? How might they view you?

- ◆ How do *you* balance the tension between recognizing that others may desperately need your help and respecting those same people as partners and leaders?

Humility

A fourth phase occurs when our eyes turn to our coworkers, or to institutions that threaten to undermine progress. We look to others across history who have undertaken similar work, with similar enthusiasm. We realize not only that their work has been incomplete but that ours, like theirs, is also likely to be incomplete. Despite our best efforts, plans will be abandoned, partners will prove unreliable, problems will recur, things will not get done. In this phase we cultivate a durable commitment that is able, perhaps for the first time, to acknowledge the goals that, realistically, we have and will accomplish, and to acknowledge these with tranquility rather than shame — or pride.

Neither we nor our generation are going to change the world completely or forever. One week after we retire there will be a staff meeting with our replacement. As someone gives a well-prepared and much-prayed-over talk on poverty and the MDGs, a child in the front row will still complain and someone in the audience will fall asleep. Somewhere a war will be starting, and somewhere else a person will be trying to steal philanthropic funds. Even if we achieve the greatest accomplishments that were feasible for us, within the next decade there will be human rights abuses and further poverty campaigns, dismal economic policies, environmental disasters, another burst of energy to reduce global poverty, a new wave of strategic planning, a technological breakthrough, and a set of inspired teenagers giving their lives to old causes as if they had just discovered them. When people see this — really grasp it — it can unseat their enthusiasm. One development worker had been working in a country for twenty years. Then, in a few months, a political turmoil undid all that he had spent his life trying to nurture. He became embittered, taciturn, grudging. He stayed in the job because it was all he knew, but his hope had shriveled.

This is a difficult phase. It is the one in which many people become disillusioned and drop away or lose interest. Part of the reason that they give up is that their hopes for what they might have achieved may have been overstated. Partly they may not be able to see what, if anything, they have actually achieved, and the work, which once seemed so fulfilling and meaningful, now feels monotonous and boring. As Melba Maggay noted, "There is something about the daily exposure to poverty and other ills of society which tends to tear away faith and make agents of change some of the most cynical people around."[3]

Also, deep down, many feel that if they were utterly available and open to God, they could be God's vessels in the world; Jesus healed people but *so did Jesus' disciples*. The disciples did great acts of power. So, many quietly think, might I. Rather than ridiculing these feelings which grow out, as it were, of God's yearning *for* people to act, and our willingness to respond utterly, we must sit alongside them and listen.

So a good place to start, when reflecting on the struggle of how to act powerfully but realistically, is humility. Humility is self-honesty, because the focus of humility is no longer you. Humility probes, searches, and marvels. But humility does not make anyone out to be more talented or powerful than he or she is. It notes and accepts limitations. A person may be soft-spoken but not timid; earnest though not witty; as graceful as a butterfly but unable to catch a beach ball. And humility is often accompanied by a generous sense of humor — a word of the same etymological origin!

Humble people recognize that they are not going to change the world forever. Whether or not they have a significant impact is partly chance and circumstance. But they certainly can do something genuinely new and genuinely valuable. They can be a part of God's acting in the world today — a space in which God acts, love is rendered, and a greater light shines through. However glib that may sound, it would be beautiful — and enough.

Thomas Merton, a twentieth-century contemplative monk, wrote an elegant sequence of thoughts on humility and faith:

---

3. Cited in Bryant L. Myers, *Walking with the Poor: Principles and Practices of Transformational Development* (Maryknoll, N.Y.: Orbis Books, 1999).

A humble man [or woman] can do great things with an uncommon perfection because he is no longer concerned about accidentals — like his own interests and his own reputation — and therefore he no longer needs to waste his efforts in defending them.

For a humble man is not afraid of failure. In fact he is not afraid of anything, even of himself, since perfect humility implies perfect confidence in the power of God, before Whom no other power has any meaning and for Whom there is no such thing as an obstacle.[4]

If you talk with seasoned activists — those who have weathered campaigns and movements and hopes and failures — and if you ask them how they deal with the recurrent setbacks, the resources they draw on are remarkably similar to Merton's. They may not sound spiritual at first glance — but they are. One organizer, who worked with Cesar Chavez's famous United Farm Workers movement in the US, liked to refer to a poem, "To Be of Use," by Marge Piercy. She writes:

> I love people who harness themselves, an ox to a heavy cart,
> who pull like water buffalo, with massive patience,
> who strain in the mud and the muck to move things forward,
> who do what has to be done, again and again. . . .[5]

The late Mahbub ul Haq, a Pakistani economist who pioneered the annual *Human Development Reports* of the United Nations, was not only an eloquent spokesman but also a poet. One of his poetry translations — which is more of a rewrite than a literal rendition — is of "Elusive Dawn" by perhaps Pakistan's greatest twentieth-century poet, Faiz Ahmad Faiz. It is the poem that we began this chapter with, and it opens by saying this:

> This trembling light, this night-bitten Dawn
> This is not the Dawn we awaited for so long

The poem then tells the story of the struggle — started generations ago, when "our hopes were young, our goal within reach." "Many seductive pleasures beckoned us on the way. But we stayed faithful to our distant dream." Again and again the friends were told that they had arrived and should stop struggling and settle down. With grim determination, they resist these voices: "let us keep marching, my tiring friends: We have yet to find our elusive Dawn."

---

4. Thomas Merton, *New Seeds of Contemplation* (New York: New Directions, 1972), 190.

5. Marge Piercy, *Circles on the Water: Selected Poems* (New York: Alfred A. Knopf, 1982).

The "elusive Dawn," the day that the mucky tasks are done, will be in the reign of God. We will not reach it in our lifetimes. In this world we actually need to keep going. Perhaps this is why Mother Teresa prayed, "Give me a vision of faith, Dear Jesus, that my work may not be monotonous."

Dependence

Humility leaves unaddressed our sinking feeling of disillusion as we gaze back across history. This book has argued that we face an unprecedented opportunity to make a historic change in the conditions of the poor — and that such changes are, empirically and politically, feasible. So why then, in our era, do we need to talk about drudgery and "elusive dawns"? Was this not a feature of the past alone?

Theologically, our work is more stable when we *are* disillusioned, when we understand that justice achievements are likely to be unstable, partial, and require constant vigilance. Even if we were to meet the MDGs by the end of 2015, there's still January 2016. Even if we were to end poverty by 2025, further problems would have emerged — with the environment, or with new diseases. This takes us to the last phase, which is dependence.

People who are dependent on God still act with passion and vigor; they still speak out; they still weep; they still urge others to take action. But they do so now, somehow, with a peculiar kind of realism or detachment from what they accomplish. It can be hard to understand at first. To some, dependence has a bad reputation — we think of alcohol or drug dependence. But think instead of how the Dutch spiritual writer Henri Nouwen described a man with this quality:

> In everything he seems to have a concrete and living goal in mind, the realization of which is of vital importance. Yet he himself maintains a great inner freedom in the light of this goal. Often it seems as though he knows that he will never see the goal achieved, and that he only sees the shadow of it himself.[6]

So, as we said earlier, maturity in the life of social justice mirrors maturity in the spiritual life. For it entails a deep shift from reliance on oneself, or on one's community, to dependence on God. God must provide for both the vision and the results. In fact, people come to rely not on what they can do by their own actions but on God. They learn

---

6. Henri Nouwen, *With Open Hands* (Notre Dame, Ind.: Ave Maria Press, 1972), 134.

to be receptive to God's guidance — "Not I, but God in me," as St. Paul puts it (1 Corinthians 15:10).

Dependence is the only place to go once we realize that there's an absolute imperative to act, but nothing we can do can change the world overnight. We're part of something bigger, and all we can do is offer something into it. We can say, with the psalmist:

> Unless the Lord builds the house,
>   those who build it labor in vain.
> Unless the Lord guards the city,
>   the guard keeps watch in vain.
>   (Psalm 127:1)

Mature activists rest in God, open and receptive to God's guidance. Insofar as they act, they act ardently. One person who exemplified this was the inspirational secretary-general of the United Nations Dag Hammarskjöld. During his lifetime he established a reputation as a determined and effective diplomat. After his untimely death in a plane crash it emerged that he kept a spiritual journal, which was later published under the title *Markings*. This book provides a remarkable insight into the spirituality of Hammarskjöld and leaves us a legacy of insights for those who work in public life and for social justice. For example, Hammarskjöld wrote, "In our era, the road to holiness necessarily passes through the world of action."[7] Yet at the same time he reflects on his dependence upon God in all that he does. This not only sustained him in his demanding role, it also put his role and his efforts into perspective, for when people recognize that success is not in their hands, it frees them from self-importance — as well as from panic. Hammarskjöld writes in this way of his relationship with God and how it transforms his professional work:

> Thou takest the pen — and the lines dance. Thou takest the flute — and the notes shimmer. Thou takest the brush — and the colours sing. So all things have meaning and beauty in that space beyond time where Thou art. How, then, can I hold back anything from Thee?[8]

To depend upon God is to recognize that God's love is the source of our own. Like Hammarskjöld we can — and, given the challenges around us, must — return again and again to God in order for hope to

---

7. Dag Hammarskjöld, *Markings* (New York: Ballantine Books, 1983), 103.
8. Ibid., 100.

be rekindled and light restored. However we do this — and it will vary for different people and at different points of life — we may come to know that this is the core of life. Because God's love is the pilot light of our own love. And it's never going to go out.

?? QUESTIONS FOR DISCUSSION

◆ What phases have you gone through? In which order have you gone through them?

Compassion — "Suffering with" — I feel others' pain and cannot turn away.

Responsibility — We can act and must — and God calls us as coworkers to serve.

Respect — The poor are leaders too, with personalities and opinions and talents!

Humility — All of my life can be given in love, but earth will still not become heaven.

Dependence — Not I, but God in me; unless the Lord builds the house. . . .

Conclusion: Spiritual renewal

Often those who are committed to social causes including poverty re-duction are described as "activists." It is tempting to contrast them with "contemplatives" — people who are prayerful, deep, and devout. Better to blend both. The story that comes to mind is that of Martha and Mary (Luke 10:38–42). While Martha busied herself with "her many tasks," Mary sat at Jesus' feet, listening to the rabbi, which was not the custom for women of the time. Jesus commended Mary for this (perhaps while tucking into Martha's lunch!), saying that Mary had chosen "the better part." That would seem to suggest that activists have chosen the inferior part and consigned themselves to being shallower and less devout. But in the words of Dorothee Soelle, "Believe me, Martha and Mary need to be together to host the Lord and keep him with them forever, or else he will be badly hosted and be left without food."[9]

In this chapter we have argued that the work of poverty reduction can deepen and renew people spiritually, and spiritual renewal in turn builds

---

9. Dorothee Soelle, *The Silent Cry: Mysticism and Resistance,* trans. Barbara and Martin Rumscheidt (Minneapolis: Fortress Press, 2001), 201.

an enduring foundation for poverty reduction. Many people are drawn to poverty reduction not by faith but for reasons of compassion or an innate sense of human concern and moral obligation. This can also be the case for people of faith, who may compartmentalize their religious convictions as separate from their economic, social, and political activities. Churches, too, may not teach about global poverty, nor encourage members to respond to problems beyond the local community. But there is a wealth of theological, economic, and spiritual connections we can make between the Christian faith and the global context of inequality and deprivation in which we live. Making these connections can help us to sustain a balance between action and contemplation, faith and works.

Discerning what one person can do requires an understanding of how one person fits into the mission of God. As the prayer below observes, "We are workers, not master builders." The poignant and beautiful incompleteness about what any one person can do contrasts with the power of what many "one persons" can do.

ACTION 8:
WHAT CAN ONE PERSON DO?
A SHOWER OF SUGGESTIONS

In the previous chapters we have identified and described seven actions or types of actions that one person can do and that could make a disproportionate difference. In this section, we broaden these, and while we include all of the points made in other chapters, we add similar activities. Of course this is not exhaustive; you or your family or coffee club might wish to brainstorm your own list of what you could do. And, as in each action previously, you might try to ascertain what particularly the action might be, why it might be strategic, what information you would require, and how, very concretely, you might do it.

Pray

1. Pray at church about working to end poverty. For example, take one MDG a week and pray for it.

2. Use an international cycle of prayer for your denomination to pray for different parts of the church every day or week.

3. Look up the information from a source such as the Human Development Report (*www.undp.org/hdr*), then pray for one country and issue a week (e.g., one week pray for the people of Tanzania,

one-third of whom are HIV-positive, then the people of Pakistan, 57 percent of whom have not had a primary school education).

4. Pray for the Global Call to Action, and the Christians and churches that are participating in it, that this will be an opportunity to renew the churches and serve those in distress.

5. Join the Micah Challenge Prayer series, which sends out prayer requests each Friday.

6. Look up "prayers for development," "prayers for peace," and "prayers for an end to hunger" in the library or on the Internet, and use these with your youth group or in church.

7. Pray for the organization(s) or people to whom you give money and for those they serve.

8. Cut out pictures or artwork of people in joyful and painful conditions in different countries, then hand them around a group. Let the pictures draw you into prayer.

Study

1. Meet with others regularly before or after church for an hour to discuss one or two current issues in the Sunday paper from the light of faith.

2. Start a book study group around a book concerning an MDG issue.

3. Invite someone to give an educational talk on the MDGs and 0.7 percent giving.

4. Download an annotated PowerPoint presentation on the MDGs (e.g., on *www.e4gr.org*), study it, and give the educational talk yourself!

5. Pick one MDG or issue (such as maternal mortality), or one country, and spend an hour a week — or a day a month — reading the booklist in Action 3 or other materials on it. There are also many speeches and videos on the Internet that you can browse!

6. Rent a movie that raises issues of poverty or inequality and have a group discussion afterward.

7. Buy a globe or large wall map of the world and learn about a new country from time to time. Mark the ones you've done!

8. Tell your neighbor, sister, colleague, mother-in-law, best friend, husband, wife, softball coach, cricket coach a bit of what you've learned.

A World without Walls

It helps now and then to step back
and take a long view.
The Kingdom is not only beyond our efforts;
it is even beyond our vision.
We accomplish in our lifetime only a tiny fraction
of the magnificent enterprise that is God's work.
Nothing we do is complete,
which is another way of saying
that the Kingdom always lies beyond us.
No statement says all that could be said,
no prayer fully expresses our faith,
no confession brings perfection,
no pastoral visit brings wholeness,
no program accomplishes the church's mission,
no set of goals and objectives includes everything.
That is what we are about.
We plant seeds that one day will grow.
We water seeds already planted,
knowing that they hold future promise.
We lay foundations that will need further development.
We cannot do everything,
and there is a sense of liberation in realizing that.
This enables us to do something and do it very well.
It may be incomplete, but it is a beginning, a step along the way
and an opportunity for the Lord's grace to enter and do the rest.
We may never see the end results,
but that is the difference
between the master builder and the worker.
We are workers, not master builders,
ministers, not messiahs.
We are prophets of a future not our own.
Amen.[a]

---

a. This prayer is usually attributed to Archbishop Oscar Romero but was actually written by Bishop Kenneth Untener of Saginaw in 1979. He wrote it for Cardinal John Dearden to offer in a Mass for deceased priests in the diocese. *National Catholic Reporter*, March 28, 2004.

9. Prod your neighbor, friend, sister, colleague, mother-in-law, best friend, husband, wife, football coach, pastor for their own thoughts on global poverty.

10. Follow the MDGs in the news for a month.

11. Give your child's teachers Web sites or details of how the class can do projects on MDG issues around the globe. Make sure they have a world map or globe!

12. If there is a tragic incident such as a tsunami, raise money to help children in affected countries — and also learn more about their countries and lives.

13. Have space in every parish and diocesan newsletter that talks about the MDGs — and what is being done about them by churches.

14. Make educational materials on the MDGs visible and available in your church.

15. Preach on the MDGs (a boilerplate sermon and examples are available at *www.e4gr.org*).

16. Lead a Bible study on poverty and a Christian response.

17. Invite students or colleagues who have traveled, lived, or worked in poor communities to tell their stories to you and your congregation.

18. Link MDG sites to your church's Web site. One possibility might be *www.developmentgoals.org.*

19. Educate church leaders about the MDGs and provide materials for them so they can preach about our unique opportunity to live as global Christians.

20. Read biographies of people who lived inspirational lives of service. They had the same number of hours in a day as you or I. How did they do it?

Give

1. Give 0.7 percent of your family's income every year to reduce global poverty.

2. Propose that your church, or other group, make a commitment to giving 0.7 percent to poverty-reducing activities. Use the proposal to educate the group as to why this is important. And make sure they enjoy the process of deciding where to give!

3. Instead of buying gifts at a store for Christmas or birthdays, give gift cards of donations to organizations working to reduce extreme

poverty (*globalgiving.org* and Heifer do this). Or buy Fair Trade gifts from online shops.

4. Have a church fund drive and solicit doctors to get materials needed to make AIDS kits, then have an afternoon of assembling and packaging them. Include notes, or have the Sunday school include pictures and letters. (At the time of writing, a list of the contents of AIDS kits can be downloaded from the Mennonite Central Committee *www.mcc.org/aids/kits/*).

5. Have every household in your parish collect pennies in jars (kids love doing this), then have a "penny harvest" every six months with the proceeds being split between local outreach and international development.

6. Do a fund-raising activity and then let the fund-raisers decide where to send the money! Help them to find certain sites — like *globalgiving.org* — discuss considerations, and choose a project. You could have all Sunday school classes do this and invite each class to make a presentation at church about their decision.

7. Get some Monopoly money together. Ask everyone in a group to calculate 0.7 percent of their income and put it into an unmarked envelope. Count the total amount of money you would have.

8. When beggars come up to your taxi window in a poor country, give to them.

9. With your loved one, go to a retreat on stewardship — such as "Ministry of Money" in the US.

10. Keep a "mite box" during Lent or Advent or a month of your choice. Add a small amount every day, and donate the contents.

11. Leave a legacy to a development agency in your will.

Connect

1. Organize a church work trip to a low-income country, connecting with the church there. Go as pilgrims walking on holy ground and listen to stories of both hope and suffering; share your lives, and work on a project that is of need to them.

2. If your church has a summer camp, look into possibilities of bringing children from another country to camp one summer (a Lutheran camp in North Carolina does this with young people from Malawi every summer).

3. Explore whether there is an organization that can use your professional skills abroad. For example RedR trains volunteer technical experts, makes agreements with their employers, and invites them to serve when emergency situations arise (*www.RedR.org*). Of course you can always refuse if the timing is wrong — there will be another time.

4. Help to support a young person who wants to spend the summer overseas, and when they come back listen to their stories and help them to sort through their experiences.

5. Seek out a grassroots immersion program to go and experience life with the poor. Resources on these are listed in Action 4.

6. The next time your family signs up for a package holiday, consider doing "community-based tourism" where you go, stay in a village, go with villagers to visit their herds, or work in their fields. Sites such as *www.responsibletourism.com* can help you get started.

7. Take an environmentally friendly holiday.

8. If you go to a developing country on business, take an extra day and find a place to visit that you wouldn't ordinarily — perhaps the local church, perhaps a project run by Oxfam or Christian Aid, perhaps a neighborhood. You might want to write about it on the plane home.

9. Learn some simple friendly greetings in another language and try them out in a developing country.

Raise awareness

1. Attend an awareness-raising concert about global poverty and take a friend.

2. Listen to music from a developing country and learn about the people.

3. Learn your favorite song related to poverty reduction and sing it everywhere.

4. Teach your children songs from other countries and songs about our connectedness with other children.

5. Buy a book of hymns and songs about unity, poverty, and generosity, and use them regularly in church and fellowship groups.

6. Write a prayer and set it to music.

7. Play some thought-provoking music before a group discussion or service.

8. Organize a "Micah Sunday" (*www.micahchallenge.org*) in your church.

Take action

1. Have a vigil or prayer service to pray for global leaders meeting to make economic decisions. Give people candles to take home and keep the light burning.

2. Go to the Global Call for Action Web site; identify and join a symbolic gathering or event.

3. Wear a white armband on key days (e.g., September 10, December 10 in 2005), and be prepared to answer people's questions as to why you are doing so (*www.whitearmband.org*).

4. Tie a white "armband" around your church's bell tower, or around your spire, to signify a public commitment to meet the MDGs.

5. Get a group together and take a bus to a large march or symbolic event related to poverty. Spend the journey and time together learning more about the issues.

6. Have the Sunday school make and sell white armbands.

Advocate

1. Find out how your representative has voted and what his or her positions are on poverty-related issues.

2. As a symbol of your faith commitment to the MDGs, sign the Micah Call (*www.micahchallenge.org*).

3. As a symbol of your commitment to the MDGs as a citizen and person of faith, sign the Make Poverty History Campaign (in the UK — *www.makepovertyhistory.org*) or the ONE Campaign (in the US — *www.onecampaign.org*).

4. Join a mailing list and write a letter or an e-mail or telephone your representative once a month.

5. Ask candidates for political office and elected officials their plans to fulfill our promises for the MDGs and related goals.

6. If your church or its members have started to give 0.7 percent, write letters to your elected representatives urging them likewise to increase funding for the MDGs.

7. Have a dinner party in which everyone writes, addresses, and stamps letters regarding a national decision on ODA or debt or trade. Mail the letters.

8. Put your church on one of the mailing lists mentioned in Action 7 and display their materials prominently.

9. Most MPs and congressional representatives have "visiting hours" every couple of weeks. Organize a group from your community, workplace, or church to visit your representative and talk with him or her about the MDGs.

10. Write a short article for your local paper that mentions the representative by name; when it comes out, send it to your representative with a cover letter.

11. Have a friend over who is in a position of political leadership; share some of your hopes and listen to their thoughts on global poverty.

12. Attend a town hall meeting or forum where you can ask your elected official(s) about the MDGs.

13. Arrange for church leaders in your town to meet with the local newspaper editorial board about the MDGs.

Others

1. Take bicycles or public transport whenever possible and planes as rarely as possible, for the former use less energy and reduce carbon emissions.

2. Try reverse haggling in a charity shop and pay more for what you buy.

3. Recycle your spectacles and help those with poor vision in the developing world (visit *www.vao.org.uk*).

4. Read *Change the World for a Fiver* (London: Short Books, 2004) and discover fifty more easy ways to make the world a better place.

Epilogue

How will our grandchildren see us?

The courageousness of a generation — or its oversights and omissions — may be starkly visible to those who come afterward. We look back on the anti-slavery movement, the struggle against apartheid, and the collapse of repressive Communist regimes in Eastern Europe and salute the courage of those who led change and those who supported the changes. We do not doubt that the changes they introduced were positive, ethical, healthy, prophetic. But at the time itself, the issues seemed far more complex — indeed, were more complex. Committed people of faith held conflicting views of how to proceed, and many were undecided or simply inactive. Action was tedious and repetitive, and at times the chances of accomplishing the goals seemed slim.

Yet in retrospect, the changes, when they came, seemed almost natural, inevitable, and irreversible. Will we look back in the same way on extreme poverty and recognize that the seemingly intractable and complex problems required most of all the will and commitment of a movement of people to effect the change?

How will our grandchildren see us? Christians love to hear about the inspiring role of the church in social change — but are more reluctant to acknowledge culpable inactions, whether they occur in South Africa, where churches supported as well as opposed apartheid; or the Rwandan genocide, where Christians actively participated; or in the Holocaust, where the response of Christians ranged from sacrificial resistance to inaction to complicity with Nazism.

Alfred Delp, a Jesuit who was executed by the Nazis for his social stance, argued that churches need to take the lead again:

> Personally I believe that unless we voluntarily stride out across new ground, leaving the well-worn paths, history-in-the-making will destroy us with a thunderbolt of judgement. And that applies both to the personal destiny of the individual churchmen and to the religious institutions as a whole.... The plundered human victim lies

192

bleeding by the wayside — must it be a stranger that comes to the rescue?[1]

We cite these examples only to observe that our actions, be they courageous or incomprehensible, are recorded and observed. *"In the evening of life, you will be examined in love,"* wrote St. John of the Cross. How will we, the 2 billion Christians now alive in the world, and our friends and neighbors fare in that examination?

Momentous challenges confront the present generation. Those who come after us will read the pages of history that we leave behind, and our response to these challenges will be plainly visible to them. We know this — and sometimes we dread it. For many of us feel powerless to affect what is written on those pages, to make a difference, to live out our values, to serve "the least of these." Yet this book joins with many others to argue that we could leave a different legacy, one that will lift the hearts of those who look back on us and rekindle their own hope. No one person could do so alone, but one person can do much in collaboration with others. Our hope, our prayer, our plea is that together we will show to our grandchildren, the impoverished, and the international community, what faith can do to mend a broken world.

---

1. *The Prison Meditations of Father Delp* (New York: Herder and Herder, 1963), written before his execution on February 5, 1945.

The Millennium Development Goals and Their Associated Targets

Goal 1: Eradicate extreme poverty and hunger

Target 1: To halve, between 1990 and 2015, the proportion of people whose income is less than $1 a day.

Target 2: To halve, between 1990 and 2015, the proportion of people who suffer from hunger.

Goal 2: Achieve universal primary education

Target 3: To ensure that, by 2015, children everywhere, boys and girls alike, will be able to complete a full course of primary schooling.

Goal 3: Promote gender equality and empower women

Target 4: To eliminate gender disparity in primary and secondary education, preferably by 2005 and in all levels of education no later than 2015.

Goal 4: Reduce child mortality

Target 5: To reduce by two-thirds, between 1990 and 2015, the under-five mortality rate.

Goal 5: Improve maternal health

Target 6: To reduce by three-quarters, between 1990 and 2015, the maternal mortality ratio.

Goal 6: Combat HIV/AIDS, malaria, and other diseases

Target 7: To have halted by 2015 and begun to reverse the spread of HIV/AIDS.

Target 8: To have halted by 2015 and begun to reverse the incidence of malaria and other major diseases.

Goal 7: Ensure environmental sustainability

Target 9: To integrate the principles of sustainable development into country policies and programs and reverse the loss of environmental resources.

Target 10: To halve by 2015 the proportion of people without sustainable access to safe drinking water and basic sanitation.

Target 11: To have achieved by 2020 a significant improvement in the lives of at least 100 million slum dwellers.

Goal 8: Develop a global partnership for development

Target 12: To develop further an open, rule-based, predictable, nondiscriminatory trading and financial system (includes a commitment to good governance, development, and poverty reduction — both nationally and internationally).

Target 13: To address the special needs of the least-developed countries (includes tariff- and quota-free access for exports, enhanced program of debt relief for and cancellation of official bilateral debt, and more generous official development assistance for countries committed to poverty reduction).

Target 14: To address the special needs of landlocked countries and small island developing states (through the Program of Action for the Sustainable Development of Small Island Developing States and 22nd General Assembly provisions).

Target 15: To deal comprehensively with the debt problems of developing countries through national and international measures in order to make debt sustainable in the long term.

Target 16: To develop and implement, in cooperation with developing countries, strategies for decent and productive work for youth.

Target 17: To provide, in cooperation with pharmaceutical companies, access to affordable essential drugs in developing countries.

Target 18: To make available, in cooperation with the private sector, the benefits of new technologies, especially information and communications technologies.

Bibliography

Adams, Marilyn McCord. *Horrendous Evils and the Goodness of God.* Ithaca, N.Y.: Cornell University Press, 1999.

Ashwin, Angela. *The Book of a Thousand Prayers.* London: Marshall Publishing, 1996.

Barrett, David, George T. Kurian, and Todd M. Johnson. *World Christian Encyclopedia: A Comparative Survey of Churches and Religions in the Modern World.* 2nd ed. Oxford and New York: Oxford University Press, 2001.

Barton, John. *Love Unknown: Meditations on the Death and Resurrection of Jesus.* London: SPCK, 1990.

Bayes, Jonathan. "William Wilberforce: His Impact on Nineteenth-Century Society." *The Churchman* 108, no. 2 (1994).

Bell, Daniel, M. *Liberation Theology after the End of History: The Refusal to Cease Suffering.* London and New York: Routledge, 2001.

Blauw, Johannes. *The Missionary Nature of the Church.* New York: McGraw-Hill, 1962.

Blomberg, Craig L. *Neither Poverty nor Riches: A Biblical Theology of Possessions.* New Studies in Biblical Theology 7. Leicester: Apollos, 1999.

Boff, Leonardo, and Clodovis Boff. *Introducing Liberation Theology.* Maryknoll, N.Y.: Orbis Books, and Tunbridge Wells, UK: Burns & Oates, 1987.

Bosch, David J. *Transforming Mission: Paradigm Shifts in Theology of Mission.* Maryknoll, N.Y.: Orbis Books, 1991.

Celebrating Resistance: The Way of the Cross in Latin America. London: Mowbray-Cassell, 1993.

Chester, Tim, ed. *Justice, Mercy and Humility: Integral Mission and the Poor.* Carlisle, UK, and Waynesboro, Ga.: Paternoster Press, 2002.

Curtis, Mark. *Trade for Life: Making Trade Work for Poor People.* London: Christian Aid, 2001.

Delp, Alfred. *The Prison Meditations of Father Delp.* New York: Herder and Herder, 1963.

Douglas, Ian T. "Anglicans Gathering for God's Mission: A Missiological Ecclesiology for the Anglican Communion." *Journal of Anglican Studies* 2, no. 2 (December 2004).

Douglas, Ian T. "Baptized into Mission: Ministry and Holy Orders Reconsidered," *Sewanee Theological Review* 40, no. 4 (Michaelmas 1997): 431–43.

Douglas, Ian T. *Fling Out the Banner: The National Church Ideal and the Foreign Mission of the Episcopal Church.* New York: Church Hymnal Corporation, 1996.

Douglas, Ian T., Richard Parker, Jeffrey Rowthorn, and Arthur Walmsley. "Why We Are Meeting." Unpublished mimeo, 2002.

Drèze, Jean, and Amartya Sen. *Hunger and Public Action.* Oxford: Clarendon Press, 1986.

Ellacuría, Ignacio, and Jon Sobrino, eds. *Mysterium Liberationis: Fundamental Concepts of Liberation Theology.* Maryknoll, N.Y.: Orbis Books, 1993.

Elliot, Charles. *Praying the Kingdom: Towards a Political Spirituality.* London: Darton, Longman and Todd, 1985.

Ferm, Deane William. *Third-World Liberation Theologies: An Introductory Survey.* Eugene, Ore.: Wipf and Stock, 1986.

Food and Agriculture Organization (FAO). *The State of Food Insecurity in the World.* Rome: FAO, 2004.

Footsteps. London: Tearfund, 2005.

Gibran, Kahlil. *The Prophet.* New York: Knopf, 1923.

Grisez, Germain, Joseph Boyle, and John Finnis. "Practical Principles, Moral Truths, Ultimate Ends." *American Journal of Jurisprudence* 32 (1987): 99–151.

Griswold, Frank. *Going Home: An Invitation to Jubilee.* Cambridge, Mass.: Cowley Publications, 2001.

Gutiérrez, Gustavo. "Liberation Praxis and Christian Faith." In *Frontiers of Theology in Latin America,* ed. Rosino Gibellini. Maryknoll, N.Y.: Orbis Books, 1979; London: SCM Press, 1980.

Gutiérrez, Gustavo. *A Theology of Liberation.* Maryknoll, N.Y.: Orbis Books, 1973.

Hammarskjöld, Dag. *Markings.* New York: Ballantine Books, 1983.

Hick, John. *Evil and the God of Love.* London: Fontana, 1968.

Hoppe, Leslie J. *There Shall Be No Poor among You: Poverty in the Bible.* Nashville: Abingdon Press, 2004.

Hunter, Susan. *Black Death: AIDS in Africa.* New York: Palgrave Macmillan, 2003.

John Paul II, *Redemptor Hominis.* London: Catholic Truth Society, 1979.

Journal of the Proceedings of the Bishops, Clergy and Laity of the Protestant Episcopal Church in the United States of America in a General Convention, 1835. New York: Swords, Stanford and Company, 1935.

Kesselus, Kenneth. " 'Awake, Thou Spirit of the Watchmen,' John E. Hines's Challenge to the Episcopal Church," *Anglican and Episcopal History* 64, no. 3. 1995.

King, Jr., Martin Luther. "Strength to Love." In *A Testament of Hope: The Essential Writings and Speeches of Martin Luther King Jr.* San Francisco and London: Harper & Row, 1986.

Leech, Kenneth. *We Preach Christ Crucified.* Cambridge, Mass.: Cowley Publications, 1984.

Llewellyn, Robert. *Prayer and Contemplation.* London: Marshall Publishing, 1989.

Mandela, Nelson. "Make History. Make Poverty History." speech given February 3, 2005, at Trafalgar Square, London. Full text available at *www.surefish.co.uk/ campaigns/mph/030205_mph_mandela_speech.htm.*

Marable, Manning. "The Case for Divestment." *The Witness* 68, no. 6 (June 1985).

Marshall Howse, Ernest. *Saints in Politics.* Toronto: University of Toronto Press, 1952.

Marshall, Katherine, and Lucy Keough. *Mind, Heart, and Soul in the Fight against Poverty.* Washington, D.C.: World Bank, 2004.

Marshall, Katharine, and Richard Marsh, eds., *Millennium Challenges for Development and Faith Institutions.* Washington D.C.; World Bank, 2003.

Massie, Robert. *Loosing the Bonds: The United States and South Africa in the Apartheid Years.* New York: Doubleday, 1997.

May, G. Lacey. *Some Eighteenth Century Churchmen.* New York: Macmillan Co., 1920.

Merton, Thomas. *New Seeds of Contemplation.* New York: New Directions, 1972.

Moltmann, Jürgen. *God for a Secular Society: The Public Relevance of Theology.* Minneapolis: Fortress Press, 1999.

Myers, Bryant L. *Walking with the Poor: Principles and Practices of Transformational Development.* Maryknoll, N.Y.: Orbis Books, 1999.

Narayan, Deepa, et al. *Can Anyone Hear Us?* Oxford: Oxford University Press, 2000.

Narayan, Deepa, et al. *Voices of the Poor: Crying Out for Change.* New York: Oxford University Press for the World Bank, 2000.

Neil, Stephen. *A History of Christian Missions.* New York: Penguin Books, 1964.

Nouwen, Henri. *With Open Hands.* Notre Dame, Ind.: Ave Maria Press, 1972.

Oduyoye, Mercy Amba, "Reflections from a Third-World Woman's Perspective: Women's Experience and Liberation Theologies." In *Feminist Theology from the Third World: A Reader,* ed. Ursula King. Maryknoll, N.Y.: Orbis Books, and London: SPCK, 1994.

The Official Report of the Lambeth Conference, 1998, Harrisburg, Pa.: Morehouse Publishing, 1999.

Piercy, Marge. *Circles on the Water: Selected Poems.* New York: Alfred A. Knopf, 1982.

Presler, Titus. *Horizons of Mission.* Cambridge, Mass.: Cowley Publications, 2001.

Ramachandra, Vinoth. "Globalization: Towards a Theological Perspective and Critique." Micah Network document published at *www.micahnetwork.org.*

Reed, Charles, ed. *Development Matters: Christian Perspectives on Globalization.* London: Church House, 2001.

Reinikka, Ritva, and Jakob Svensson. *Working for God? Evaluating Service Delivery of Religious Not-for Profit Health Care Providers in Uganda.* Center for Economic Policy and Research Discussion Paper 4214. Washington, D.C.: World Bank, 2003.

Rowland, Christopher, ed. *The Cambridge Companion to Liberation Theology.* Cambridge: Cambridge University Press, 1999.

Rough Guide to a Better World, A. Produced by the Department for International Development in the UK. Available free from post offices in the UK.

Rowthorn, J. *"Tract for Our Times,"* EGR Web page, *www.e4gr.org.*

Samartha. S. J. One *Christ — Many Religions: Towards a Revised Christology.* Maryknoll, N.Y.: Orbis Books, 1995.

Sachs, Jeff. *The End of Poverty: Economic Possibilities for Our Time.* London and New York: Penguin, 2005.

Sider, Ronald J. *Rich Christians in an Age of Hunger.* Nashville: W Publishing Group, 2005.

Sider, Ronald J., Philip N. Olson, and Heidi Rolland Unruh. *Churches That Make a Difference: Reaching Your Community with Good News and Good Works.* Grand Rapids: Baker Books, 2002.

Soares-Prabhu, George. "Class in the Bible: The Biblical Poor a Social Class?" In *Voices from the Margin: Interpreting the Bible in the Third World,* ed. R. S. Sugirtharajah. London: SPCK, 1991.

Soelle, Dorothee. *The Silent Cry: Mysticism and Resistance.* trans. Barbara and Martin Rumscheidt. Minneapolis: Fortress Press, 2001.

Soelle, Dorothee. *Suffering.* Trans. Everett Kalin. Philadelphia: Fortress Press, 1975.

Senior, David, and Carol Stuhlmueller. *The Biblical Foundations for Mission.* Maryknoll, N.Y.: Orbis Books, 1984.

Stanton, Graham N. *Gospel for a New People: Studies in Matthew.* Edinburgh: T. & T. Clark, 1992.

Suárez, Margarit M. W. "Across the Kitchen Table: Cuban Women Pastors." In *Gender Ethnicity, and Religion: Views from the Other Side,* ed. Rosemary Radford Ruether. Minneapolis: Fortress Press, 2002.

Sustainable Human Development: A Young People's Introduction. London: Peace Child International, 2002.

Tamez, Elsa. "Women's Rereading of the Bible." In *Voices from the Margin: Interpreting the Bible in the Third World,* ed. R. S. Sugirtharajah. London: SPCK, 1991.

Taylor, Michael. *Poverty and Christianity: Reflections at the Interface between Faith and Experience.* London: SCM Press, 2000.

United Nations Development Program. *Human Development Report.* New York: Oxford University Press, 2003.

United Nations Development Program. *Investing in Development: A Practical Plan to Achieve the Millennium Development Goals.* London: Earthscan, 2005.

Wallis, Jim. "The Power of Hope: A Sign of Transformation." *Sojourners Magazine* (September–October 1994).

Wallis, Jim. *God's Politics: Why the Right Gets It Wrong and the Left Doesn't Get It.* San Francisco: HarperCollins, 2005.

Williams, Jessica. *50 Facts That Should Change the World.* Thriplow, UK: Icon Books, 2004.

Wink, Walter. *Engaging the Powers: Discernment and Resistance in a World of Domination.* Minneapolis: Fortress Press, 1992.

Williams, Rowan. *Open to Judgment: Sermons and Addresses.* London: Darton, Longman and Todd, 1984.

World Bank. *Millennium Development Goals: From Consensus to Momentum,* Global Monitoring Report. Washington, D.C.: World Bank, 2005.

Contributors

The Rev. Dr. Sabina Alkire is an economist, research associate at the Global Equity Initiative, Harvard University, and a nonstipendiary priest at St. Stephen's South End, Boston. She is the author of *Valuing Freedoms* (Oxford University Press, 2002).

The Rev. Dr. Edmund Newell is canon chancellor of St. Paul's Cathedral, London, and founding director of the St. Paul's Institute, a forum for education and debate on issues of faith, ethics, and the global economy. He was formerly research fellow in economic history at Nuffield College, Oxford.

Ann Barham is a freelance writer, researcher, and playwright based in Washington, D.C. She has worked on the UN's Commission on Human Security, Harvard University's Global Equity Initiative, and as a senate staffer. She is currently enrolled at Harvard Divinity School in Cambridge, Massachusetts.

The Rev. Chloe Breyer is an Episcopal priest at St. Mary's, Manhattanville, in West Harlem. A contributor to *Slate* magazine, she is also the author of *The Close: A Young Woman's First Year at Seminary* (Basic Books, 2000). From 2000 to 2003, she directed the Cathedral Forums on Religion and Public Life at the Cathedral of St. John the Divine in New York. She is involved in interfaith work in the Diocese of New York and helped lead an initiative to rebuild a mosque in Afghanistan destroyed by US bombs in November 2001.

The Rev. Ian T. Douglas, PhD, is the Angus Dun Professor of Mission and World Christianity at the Episcopal Divinity School in Cambridge, Massachusetts. A widely published missiologist, he serves on the Inter-Anglican Standing Commission on Mission and Evangelism and the Design Group for the 2008 Lambeth Conference and is also a consultant for the presiding bishop and House of Bishops of the Episcopal Church. Douglas was one of the cofounders of Episcopalians for Global Reconciliation.